Mommy Needs a Raise

(Because Quitting's Not an Option)

Other Books by Sarah Parshall Perry

Sand in My Sandwich

When the Fairy Dust Settles with Janet Parshall

Mommy
Needs
a Raise

(Because Quitting's Not an Option)

SARAH PARSHALL PERRY

Revell

a division of Baker Publishing Group
Grand Rapids, Michigan

Published by Revell
a division of Baker Publishing Group
P.O. Box 6287, Grand Rapids, MI 49516-6287
www.revellbooks.com

Printed in the United States of America

Library of Congress Cataloging-in-Publication Data
Names: Perry, Sarah Parshall, author.
Title: Mommy needs a raise : because quitting's not an option / Sarah Parshall Perry.
Description: Grand Rapids : Revell, 2016. | Includes bibliographical references.
Identifiers: LCCN 2016001654 | ISBN 9780800724115 (pbk.)
Subjects: LCSH: Mothers—Religious life. | Motherhood—Religious aspects—
    Christianity. | Working mothers. | Work and family.
Classification: LCC BV4529.18 .P468 2016 | DDC 248.8/431—dc23
LC record available at http://lccn.loc.gov/2016001654

Unless otherwise indicated, Scripture quotations are from the Holy Bible, New International Version®. NIV®. Copyright © 1973, 1978, 1984, 2011 by Biblica, Inc.™ Used by permission of Zondervan. All rights reserved worldwide. www.zondervan.com

Scripture quotations labeled ASV are from the American Standard Version of the Bible.

Scripture quotations labeled ESV are from The Holy Bible, English Standard Version® (ESV®), copyright © 2001 by Crossway, a publishing ministry of Good News Publishers. Used by permission. All rights reserved. ESV Text Edition: 2011

Scripture quotations labeled NLT are from the Holy Bible, New Living Translation, copyright © 1996, 2004, 2007 by Tyndale House Foundation. Used by permission of Tyndale House Publishers, Inc., Carol Stream, Illinois 60188. All rights reserved.

Some names and details have been changed to protect the privacy of the individuals involved.

Author is represented by Wordserve Literary, Inc., www.wordserveliterary.com

16 17 18 19 20 21 22   7 6 5 4 3 2 1

For my mother

Contents

Acknowledgments

I extend my deepest gratitude to my fabulous Revell team: Lonnie Hull DuPont, Lindsey Spoolstra, Twila Bennett, Lindsay Davis, and Claudia Marsh. I love them, and they love me back. They are the kind of people I would be friends with even if they weren't being paid to like what I do.

I want to thank my dad, Craig Parshall, for his love of books and words and for being stellar with his use of both. Because of him, I only ever wanted to write. All the pieces were there. I simply put them together.

I want to thank my mother-in-law, Sue Perry, who was the right combination of tough and tender in raising three boys, one of whom still knows well enough to open doors for me.

I want to thank my mom, Janet Parshall. She showed me just how high a calling motherhood is. Greatest thanks go to my family: my husband, Matt, and my children, Noah, Grace, and Jesse. I am grateful to them for being so awesome and passionate and unique and funny that there is enough material to fill a book about it all. Every day with them is a treasure. Their "I love yous" give me butterflies. Until our reality show is developed, this book will have to do.

Finally, I thank the Lord for the courage, wisdom, and faith—despite my weaknesses and obvious failings—to thrive in this calling of motherhood.

It's the best job I have ever had.

Prelude

This is what the LORD says. . . . "Forget the former things; do not dwell on the past. See, I am doing a new thing! Now it springs up; do you not perceive it? I am making a way in the wilderness and streams in the wasteland."

Isaiah 43:16, 18–19

one

Meet the Donners

The thing about having kids is not the stuff that you expect.

Certain things are predictable. You know to expect a certain level of sleep deprivation. You know the baby needs shots. You know that car seats are necessary, tantrums are inevitable, and baby teeth will fall out. Dr. Spock even wrote a how-to manual in the 1960s for every apprehensive parent who thought they needed a guidebook so that they'd remember the proper way to dry a baby after a bath. (For example, use a towel instead of the casual heat setting on your dryer.)

It's the stuff you *don't* expect about parenting that's really going to blow your mind. It's the way that, despite your best intentions, just about everything you've planned for yourself and this new band of little groupies is going to fly wildly off the rails—sparks flying, people screaming, engine on fire *off the rails*.

I was a parent who vowed my car would never look like the standard "kid taxi"—the one with the crushed Cheerios, the half-full juice box, the melted crayons on the floor. No, by George, I was going to use what I'm sure is my undiagnosed obsessive compulsive disorder to keep my car pristine. My kids were going to learn to clean up after themselves, and my things would not pay the price. Wouldn't they naturally understand that I was the one making the car payment, and they had to respect someone else's things?

No, they would not understand that.

The tires on my car recently had to be rotated. We were in the middle of winter, and when rounding the corner one afternoon I'd hit a puddle of slush and road salt that left a rainbow of grey sludge on the entire right side of my car. Plus, it looked like the Rolling Stones had been on a bender in the backseat. There was a hair bow near Grace's seat with no clip attached. There were also the covers for a set of headphones that she'd inexplicably removed, two broken pencils, and a travel mug whose contents had frozen solid. On Jesse's side, there were pieces of a LEGO set, a dog-eared book with pages stuck together by something unknown, and some crushed Cheez-Its. As for Noah's side, he makes it appear clean by kicking everything under the seat in front of him. So I have to regularly get behind the bench and pull out things like wrappers, art projects, sports balls, and writing utensils he swears to me he can't find. He once lost an iPad somewhere between the car and a store. A store ten feet away from where our car was parked.

On this day, I'd dropped my car off to have the tire work done, and when I returned to my car a few hours later, I gasped.

The shop had washed the car. I opened the door and saw the interior had been vacuumed as well. Do you know what I did? I screamed. *Screamed.* That is how happy I was. That is how happy you will be, too, when someone surprises you with the taste of something you once swore you'd have and, somewhere along the line, were totally surprised by the loss of. Childrearing is one of those things that looks commonplace yet its components are anything but. I have ended the previous two sentences with prepositions. That is also something I swore I would never do. But there, I have done it so that you may further realize how incredibly surprising everything is about this mothering business.

At some point in the future, you will find yourself with a dish towel in your hand after you have cleaned up from dinner. After you have taken a kitchen from nice and clean to food-smattered and dirty and back to clean again (which is the same thing you have done every day for an innumerable sum of days), you will think to yourself, *What am I doing? What's happened to me?* The very nature of this repetition will surprise you, because you will at some point believe that every day with these small people will be a miracle. And yes, it is. Because they are alive, and you have had a part in that. And they have not yet burned you in effigy because they are too young to know how, and they don't yet get that you aren't a perfect mother. Things will seem very right and very wonderful.

And very, very repetitive.

So you will wonder exactly what your particular value is to them, and to yourself, and to the world at large.

It may, just for a moment or even for a longer period of time (I will not judge you, even if it is a period of years and you struggle with telling people what it is you do for a living), feel just the tiniest bit like a wasteland. A long, flat, unchanging wasteland with the landscape altered only by the occasional punctuation of laundry mountains or bathwater rivers.

There is a point at which you may start to feel like you are a member of the ill-fated Donner party.

•   •   •   •   •

The Donner Party was a group of eighty-seven American pioneers who set out from Illinois in 1846 on a 2,500-mile journey to California. In a lengthy wagon train of families and friends, husbands laughed as they guided the oxen and little ones sang in the back and held their belongings under the snapping bonnet. Mothers clutched babies—all eager to begin the adventure before them.

However, the party made the unfortunate decision to follow a new route called the Hastings Cutoff, which traversed Utah's Wasatch Mountains and added 150 miles to their journey. The virtually impassable terrain resulted in the loss of cattle and wagons, and caused infighting and an eventual split within the party. A series of mishaps delayed the party further. By the beginning of November 1846, already delayed by nearly three weeks, the travelers reached the Sierra Nevada Mountains where they became trapped by an early and unexpected snowfall. The party became snowbound, locked in the mountains with both food stores and spirits rapidly dwindling. In December 1846, some of the men set out on foot to get help but most perished on the way. The first rescuers from California did not reach the party until February 1847, some four months after the party had become trapped. With the oxen dead and food supplies eliminated, some of the emigrants resorted to cannibalism to survive, eating those who had succumbed to starvation and sickness.

That's right. They *ate* each other.

Of the eighty-seven who had set out on the journey, only forty-eight lived to see California.

Do you know why the Donner Party took that cutoff? Because they were surprised. They were surprised by the terrain, by the mud and the mountains and the sheer length of the journey, and they took the cutoff in an attempt to survive. Do you know why they set out on foot for help? Because the surprise of an early snowfall locked half of them in the mountains after they had taken that cutoff.

Surprised.

It is worth noting here that on the journey, the death rate among males ages twenty to thirty-nine was "extremely high" at more than 66 percent.[1] This is due in part to the fact that men metabolize protein faster than women, and women don't require as high a caloric intake. Additionally, women store more body fat than men, which delays the effects of physical degradation caused by starvation and overwork. The Donner men also took on more dangerous tasks than their female counterparts: felling trees, shooting bears, throwing knives, and whatever else pioneer men did in those days, further breaking down their bodies. However, men in families tended to live longer than bachelor males, possibly owing to their willingness to share food and provide emotional support.[2]

This is good news for mothers all around. If you've ever struggled with your weight, if you're part of a family, and if you're not regularly engaged in activities like bear stabbing or brush clearing, chances are you'll live longer than your husband. I'm sure this was part of God's plan to make sure that the better-suited parent sticks around to take care of the kids.

You, hopefully, will not ever feel like you need to eat anyone to survive parenthood, but you will at some point wear something out of the house that you believe is clean until you reach into your pocket and notice that there is dried substance on your shirt. When you discover this crusty thing, it will be in public, where changing your shirt is not an option, and you realize you have once again been taken by surprise.

One thing will keep you pressing through all the surprises in the wasteland: your purpose on the journey. The worth you find in what you are doing is what will motivate you to keep doing it day in and day out, to repeat motions that may not, in the short term, appear to be for any long-term gain.

But what exactly *is* the worth in what you're doing? Whither thou, dear purpose? No one is going to tell you that you are underpaid and underappreciated. Though at some point, you may feel both. If you lack awareness of your own significance before you set your feet upon this motherhood path, the terrain will prove difficult. And I lacked that awareness. I attempted a route most often traveled by men—that of finding meaning in what I did, in my professional designation and my trade. Then I gave it up. I gave in to the daily needs of the people around me, and suddenly I found myself where you might be now, questioning my choices and my worth.

The United Nations is using a heavily researched document from Columbia University called the "World Happiness Report 2015" to develop sustainable goals across the globe.[3] This study, with contributions from experts in the fields of psychology, health, public policy, and economics, makes the startling revelation that the United States, though the fifth richest country in the world, ranks only fifteenth in global happiness. Something is wrong. "Ought not there be an increment, earned though not yet received, from one's daily work—an acknowledgement of [wo]man's *being*?"[4] Shouldn't there be value in what we do? And don't we have worth beyond it?

Maybe simply "surviving" motherhood has eliminated your perspective on your own value. Maybe you can't see the bigger picture because you are kneeling on the floor with a bucket and a rag, cleaning up your middle child's vomit. And you have to understand your value in the whole scheme of motherhood or you're going to wind up feeling like Mary Donner, who was so exhausted from the journey she accidentally burned her frostbitten feet in a campfire halfway through the trip. You may not know who you are apart from these little people or what your worth is without them. At which point, you might find yourself in the teeniest existential crisis.

I understand. I was a Mary Donner once too.

two

A Job Is a Job

Welcome.

I sincerely hope you haven't come here looking for answers. I am too dysfunctional to provide you with a missive on how to raise your kids. That's what I read *other people's* books for. I am, however, going to tell you the story of your life. I will simply use myself as a placeholder.

One of my favorite writers, Nora Ephron, once said, "When you slip on a banana peel, people laugh at you; but when you tell people you slipped on a banana peel, it's your laugh. So you become the hero rather than the victim of the joke."[1] There will be plenty of banana peels in this book, and in your interest, I will stick my neck out and say things that maybe you've never said but have sometimes thought. Because we own these stories, you and I. We own them from the day we start the journey until the day we're called home. Once we've taken the first step forward, there's no turning back. And that's part of what makes us heroes. We are mothers, after all. And if we can't laugh at ourselves or the seeming impossibility of this job of raising kids, we're in for a haul. So I'm just going to lay it all out there, m'kay?

Yesterday, I actually said out loud, "I'm done today! Today I don't want to be a mother!" The washing machine seal had busted, the kids had tracked a mud path through the house, Matt was traveling, and there was nothing to eat. Then, just as I was running the water for Jesse's bath, the shower curtain collapsed into the tub full of water. I was totally over it.

I didn't realize Jesse was behind me as I groused. I feel the need to make this point clear, because I can't think of ever being frayed enough to look my children in the eye and tell them that I wanted to "undo" motherhood. Even for a day. But Jesse, the human elf with his grandfather's lop ears, a mouth missing teeth, and a spate of freckles across his nose—sprinkled in between his dimples—laughed and said, "Well, too bad, Mama! It's your job!"

He is right. I am a writer and a lawyer. I have worked in advertising and education. I have worked in retail and public policy, but my "job" is mother. My husband does not identify himself as a father first. He will say he is in sales. But I, on the other hand, know I am defined first by the humans I've chaperoned down from the Bright Place into this world. I guard them here. They are God's lifelong calling on my life.

Ever since Eve decided a serpent was an excellent conversationalist and was evicted from Eden with her husband, it has been the lot of humankind to work. Everyone toils for what they have by the sweat of their brows, whether or not they are paid for doing so. Indeed, useful production even precedes the fall. Adam was tasked with naming the animals.

He and his wife were given stewardship over the garden; they were required "to work it and take care of it" (Gen. 2:15). There was, it seems, no original "free ride." To my mind, the critical distinction here is that in Eden, God provided everything that was needed. Humans only had to supply the stewardship, the caretaking. Now we are required to provide everything needed *and* steward it. And a fun supplement for us ladies: women get "pains in childbearing [that are] very severe; with painful labor [they] will give birth to children" (3:16). When the Creator of the universe memorializes for eternity how painful childbirth will be, you really need to start asking yourself why you're swearing off that epidural.

In general, work can be monotonous. It will, even for those passionate about what they do, prove dehumanizing at some point. Work involves the creation of something: a good, a service, some proof of production. Jobs require output. And the same output, day after day, creates a tedium of routine that can lead you to question exactly why it is you're doing the work in the first place.

In 2013, *Forbes* magazine reposted a question originally raised on Quora.com: "Why Do So Many People Hate Their Jobs?"[2] Contributors posited a number of theories. Among them: the safe path, chosen right out of school, offered security and posed a lower risk than switching gears and pursuing a passion as a career. It was remarked that "fun" jobs didn't require a salary and that doing the work itself was payment enough. But interestingly, one contributor noted that the way we evaluate jobs has changed, and now, beyond the mere security of daily survival or the hope of group identification, we advanced mammals have the opportunity for self-actualization. We can now decide whether a job is fulfilling and brings us a measure of intrinsic value. It's a question some historians theorize our ancestors didn't have the liberty to ask. But it is this value that the mother, with dish towel in chapped hand and food on dirty pants, can find herself trying to grasp: *I make people. And I take care of them. That's important, right?*

Right!?

Pulitzer Prize–winning author Studs Terkel wrote the seminal piece on value in employment. In his book, *Working*, he interviewed employees of all types, in every field of work. Terkel's work was hailed by the *Los Angeles Times* as a "celebration of individuals." The *Chicago Daily News* called it a description of the "real American experience, the poetry of real people, the hardness of real lives." Terkel sought to gauge the complexity and meaning in human existence by defining what people do.

What he discovered was this:

> It is about a search . . . for daily meaning as well as daily bread, for recognition as well as cash, for astonishment rather than torpor; in short, for a sort of life rather than a Monday through Friday sort of dying. Perhaps immortality, too, is part of the quest. To be remembered was the wish, spoken and unspoken, of the heroes and heroines. . . . There is a common attribute here: a meaning to their work well over and beyond the reward of a paycheck.[3]

There is a universal human need for something more. But this "more" seems to evade description. The notion of value, of worth or meaning, seems very arbitrary in the wasteland. It is capricious, to an extent. Consider for a moment the set of twelve gold-plated zodiac animal heads by dissident artist Ai Weiwei, which sold at auction in London last year for a staggering $4.3 million.[4] These by the same artist who famously smashed a Han dynasty urn in his 1995 performance art piece.

Someone paid $4.3 million for art by a guy whose trademark is destroying art.

My kids destroy stuff all the time, but no one's offered me a dime.

Consider also the Hermes Birkin bag. This iconic, oft-photographed handbag is hand-assembled in France and is reputed to have a wait list as long as six years (closing at random intervals so as to provoke the bag's inaccessibility). A "basic" model, the smallest of the options, carries an approximate price tag of $7,000. If your purse costs as much as something you can use to get from one place to another, methinks your priorities are out of whack. However, if I should someday come into a great sum of money, I will perhaps buy one, so don't judge. It will be strictly for research purposes. To ascertain its value.

I attended an antiques show a few weeks ago. Not one of those quaint expos where charming grannies lay out tables of colored glassware or dolls with creepy faces. They'd have done better to call this show a "landed gentry expo for people who want to buy a genuine Civil War–era flag." I'm surprised they didn't require financial statements at the door. I saw items priced as high as $35,000 and wondered why exactly I was wasting my Saturday. I wanted one small figurine. A measly token. These rich people were making it impossible. Some items came with explanations of their antiquity, setting the item into a historical context that established its worth. But some pieces bore nothing more than tags. Complicating things? The same set of Staffordshire china sheep were priced differently in two different booths—just a few steps from each other. I fought the urge to yell across the aisle that the vendors were price gouging each other. But who cared? I went home to my replicas and cracked vases—vases cracked three consecutive times by three children who consecutively decided to knock them over in the same way, despite being consecutively told that they were going to be punished if they sprinted through the dining room again.

The value of an item is only what a buyer is willing to pay. Even as arbitrarily high as some things are priced, there is someone, somewhere, who's decided that these extortionist prices are completely acceptable. These people are either flush with unused cash or essentially mean, because they're pricing the rest of us out of the market on simple things like vases we want to replace—because someone with the power to do so has slapped a tag with a random price on it and shoved normal people like us right out of the bidding.

"Pay" is essential to value. But I've learned that "pay" doesn't always mean money. Pay takes many forms. How does one value what he or she does? Does it come from making an impact or doing work about which one is passionate? Does it stem from the love of what one does? Is value synonymous with respect, or affection, or longevity in the workplace? How is one paid?

I have been compensated in many different ways. It is this changing landscape—this crossing over the divide between paycheck and people, this transition from worker to mother—that's proved one of the most challenging of my life. It's also a geography that may prove of some benefit to a mother who finds herself now wearing spit-up instead of a suit.

If you are a mother, you will probably do more of the work than your spouse. I can say this because other people, progressive people, have said it too.[5] Though childcare and breadwinning goals are "converging" in American homes, women still spend more time with their children than men.[6] A 2015 study from Ohio State University found that even for couples who said, before children, that they were planning to equally divide household responsibilities, it didn't actually develop that way after the kid was in the picture. In fact, at the nine-month postpartum mark, when both parents thought they had added thirty hours of parenthood work to their schedules, a breakdown of their time showed something completely different. "Parenthood does result in increased work . . . [and] women come close[st to 30 hours]—working 21 more hours per week after the birth of their first child. Men do much less than they—or their wives—perceive: parenthood only adds 13 hours of work for men."[7]

With over 80 percent of women becoming mothers by the age of forty-four, and about five million stay-at-home moms nationwide,[8] it basically comes down to this: we are just plain doing more of the parenting work than men.

I have an awesome husband who spends loads of time with our children. Yet he doesn't mind me saying this. He also remembers the two or two hundred minor crises I had when I realized that despite my seven years of higher education (and its accompanying debt), I was standing in the kitchen in my pajamas with dirty hair just about every day when he came home. He was returning to a house just as chaotic as the one he'd left in the morning, and I had nothing to show for the eight hours I'd lived in his absence. There were pets and children crawling around my feet and I felt like I was being sucked into the Great Pit of Carkoon by the Sarlacc sand monster in *Return of the Jedi*.

I would watch the clock, starting at 6:30 p.m., counting down the hours until I could put on my sweatpants (oh, who am I kidding, I wore them all day) and crawl into bed.

Whether you've made the transition from working woman to stay-at-home mom or you balance the two, you will have been blindsided by unexpected messes and sleeplessness and fights between siblings over stupid things like who gets the blue freeze-pop when there's only one left. You may read somewhere that there are fourteen jobs attributable to a mother and that her value in real dollars is approximately $61,436 per year.[9] You may read elsewhere that the value of a stay-at-home mom is closer to $118,000 per year.[10] *Yes*, you may think. *That's more like it.*

The interminable work of motherhood will exhaust you. The unpredictability of the small people in your house will startle you. And the dirty laundry, screaming child, snotty-nosed monotony of the wasteland mothering thing is going to make you think to yourself that you could really use a raise.

Free Range

The "work ethic" holds that labor is good in itself; that a man or woman becomes a better person by virtue of the act of working.

Richard Nixon

I put my heart and my soul into my work, and have lost my mind in the process.

Vincent van Gogh

three

Look What I Can Do

My first productive impulses were creative.

Shoot. That's not very original. I suppose every little girl digs in the dirt or draws on her little brother with a Sharpie. Let me try this again.

My first professional impulses—those upon which I could ever be called to produce anything aside from pure misery—were to write. When asked what I wanted to be when I was older, the answer was always, "A writer." Sometimes I said it with my mouth. Sometimes it just burned quietly in my heart, hiding behind the façade of a feigned interest in something more logical. But it was always there.

For a brief period, I responded to this question with, "An astrophysicist" or "A marine biologist" because I thought the old folks would be impressed with my superior intelligence at such a young age, but this was a patent overstatement of my abilities in math and science. In fact, I did take a calculus class in high school, partly because the class was an advanced placement class, and therefore weighted with more credits, which looked better on college applications. But I will tell you dragging myself through that class felt like Frodo trying to scale Mount Doom. I scraped by with a B- and a commitment to never take math again if I could possibly help it. However, if my children are reading this book, let me make clear that "Math is very important, and you need to take as much math as you possibly can. But please do not ask me to help you with your homework, because I will probably embarrass you with my not-mathing."

Advanced science classes were more interesting to me. I loved chemistry strictly for the possibility that someone might accidentally start a fire in the lab. In AP biology, I was able to work on an actual cadaver at the University of Wisconsin Medical College. It was for this reason that most of us were enrolled in this class in the first place. The med students had a great deal of fun at our expense. We came in thinking we were real cowboys until one of us was asked to hold a lung and promptly passed out.

Fine, I thought. *I didn't want your left-brain nonsense anyway.* Besides, I was born with what one might call an "artistic temperament" (which is to say I was a virtuoso of moodiness). I often tripped over things or ran into walls because I was constantly in my own head. I heard discussions between friends and wondered how they might be reproduced as dialogue. I was always searching for metaphors and for extraordinary descriptions of ordinary things. I would lie on my back in the yard, staring up at the sky and thinking big thoughts. I languished over stories and poems and jotted my own in a very private notebook that I laid out conveniently for everyone to see. I drew a little (passably). I painted a little (poorly). But it was the writing, the seeing of things and their translation to paper, the ignition of new ideas or interpretations—all of this is what kept me on the shag carpet in my room, with my feet on the wall and a book on my stomach at all hours of the day.

Yes, I thought. *That's what I want to do.*

I loved my English classes. Jack London's *White Fang* seeped into my subconscious. It impacted me enough that my eighth grade English teacher, Mrs. Pearce, wrote me a personal note telling me how much she enjoyed the short story I had written after reading it. She noted that it took some of the form and language of London's book, and wasn't that wonderful? Of course I am old enough now to recognize that this was outright plagiarism, but Mrs. Pearce was simply fanning the creative flame. I wanted to write like Gene Stratton-Porter when I read *A Girl of the Limberlost*. When I read *The Good Earth*, I imagined my writings a la Pearl S. Buck. My grandmother gave us children the complete works of Beatrix Potter, Louisa May Alcott, and Laura Ingalls Wilder, and I devoured them. A box set of books was better than a Barbie dream house.

My father will likely read this and muse that it was his reading Shakespeare to my mother's swollen belly as she lay in bed pregnant with *moi* that is to be credited with this interest. Indeed, the first piece of writing I ever memorized was one of my father's favorite poems, and one he often read to me: "When You Are Old" by William Butler Yeats. It describes a singular, pensive moment in the life of an elderly woman and her regret at having lost her one chance at true love.

Actually, the poem is kind of a downer.

Every year, my father wrote us a story and hid it in the branches of our Christmas tree. When the haze of decimated wrapping paper had been cleared, he would pull it ceremoniously from between the boughs and uncurl it from its red satin ribbon. We would sit transfixed by the soothing baritone of his voice and the tapestry he wove word by word. In later years, we knew to get up and get the Kleenex before the reading started, because it wasn't a question of whether we would cry but how soon into the story. My dad tapped the place inside us that all good writers reach: the thinking soul, the place where imagination and reality converge and we understand something for the first time, or comprehend it better because someone has beautifully, through nothing more than the expression of words, connected it for us.

So, Dad, this book is sort of your fault.

I eschewed young adult books in favor of the classics. Always have. Like I'm too good for commercial fiction. Whatever. It's not that I'm too good for it, it's just that I've tried to teach myself the best ways of writing by creating my own makeshift MFA program. This is because, at such a late date, my husband has refused to dedicate any more money to my education (seeing as I'll be paying off law school until I'm sixty). Our retirement plan is to get out of debt. Also, I have no more brain space for studying anything other than a grocery list. It's a wonder I'm able to write this book, but considering the subject matter I think you'll understand why.

The closest I came to the young adult genre was *Are You There, God? It's Me, Margaret* by Judy Blume. I don't know any woman of my age who hasn't read it, and because a few years ago it was listed among *Time* magazine's top one hundred fiction books of the past century, I am pretty comfortable calling it a classic. Chasing boys, doing home-work, and struggling with puberty are classics, anyway.

Growing up, I was nothing if not literate. Not cool, or hot, or athletic, but very, very literate.

My siblings and I were also a little wild. Not in the "break-ing curfew to go smoke at the convenience store" wild. Think, "Let's stay up late to write a play for Mom and Dad" kind of wild. Think, "My brother's in a band called 'Bob's Garage' that plays in an actual garage," kind of wild. Think, "My sister went through an emo period in which she thought wearing a cape was a good idea" kind of wild. This "wild-ness" is characteristic of artistic types. All four of us sang, played instruments, or acted in plays. My brother Sam was bitten early by the movie bug and, at thirteen, stole my par-ents' camcorder to make home movies that were more like home sagas. These were *Indiana Jones*, *Star Wars*, and *Home Alone* knockoffs requiring extensive production and editing. Music was clipped from the original and then played over the resulting product. We thumbed our noses at copyright law and enlisted neighborhood kids and friends from school to act with us. I drew the opening credit pictures and my sister constructed costumes. It was all very bohemian. I blame this on my parents. My mother, the music major, and my father, the English major, were doing theater together years before they were even married. After marriage and children, they were frequent stars in productions at our local civic theater. Watching them in *The Pirates of Penzance* and *Brigadoon* made me feel like the daughter of celebrities. They were our very own Lundts. You can't stand backstage with a bunch of stifled thirtysomethings who once took a speech class and not think you've found some magic portal to the Great

White Way. Nothing says Broadway like an actor who puts his own landscaping business in the program.

I have passed down this same rogue art gene to my children. Before typing this sentence, I got my hair caught in Noah's music stand. You see, I'd just gotten a call from school, where a penitent Noah told me he had forgotten to bring his saxophone. Again. Noah doesn't forget to bring his voice, though, which is partly why I'm encouraging him to pursue this aspect of music: it's totally portable and I won't get phone calls from school asking me to make another trip. Plus, Noah has an exceptional voice. This isn't parental exaggeration. The boy's vocal chords ring like a bell. His sister, Grace, and brother, Jesse, are likewise artistically inclined, but their talents lay in the dramatic arts. To date, this has only manifested itself in their ability to scream at the top of their lungs in very small spaces. Think black box theater for the grade school set. They've also experimented with performance art. Pouring milkshakes on themselves, public urination, things of that sort. My husband, Matt, though he has an exceptional appreciation for music and can identify a song within two bars, cannot carry a tune in a bucket with two handles. However, this does not prevent him from singing karaoke very, very loudly.

I wanted to major in English in college. I really did. But it's hard to make a living as an English major unless you go on to get a master's in fine arts, and then either (1) teach, or (2) suffer the penniless ignominy of submitting manuscript after rejected manuscript until something hits. Not being one to assume this kind of risk (or any risk, for that matter), I did what I felt was the next best thing. I majored in journalism and went on to law school. Which means I would have gone broke either way. I don't like thinking about how much *more* broke I am now. The promise of what I might earn as a lawyer was enough to bury any deep-rooted sense of anxiety about paying back Uncle Sam. (Though here I am, having to pay back Uncle Sam—and writing anyway. Between the federal government and me, I am clearly the sucker.)

Eventually, I had to move forward in the actual making of something. I briefly considered the field of journalism. I thought I was perhaps called to roving reporter status. I minored in French, thinking I'd cover Jacque Chirac's first term as president and envisioned myself eating crepes on the Seine with a jaunty beret and a thrift-shop messenger bag full of notes and press credentials. I had a poster of *The Paper*—a movie with Glenn Close, Michael Keaton, and Robert Duvall—hanging in my dorm room. *The Paper* chronicles a fast-paced twenty-four-hour period in the life of a newspaper editor. I was headed for a life reporting high-profile crimes and police cover-ups, I just knew it.

But the fascination was fleeting. I acquired many hours of practice writing news stories and editing submissions as the feature articles editor of the student newspaper. I loved the title of "editor," but was having a whit of trouble getting jazzed about relaying the opening of another Krispy Kreme donut shop. I am a creature of unrepentant subjectivity. Everything I write has an angle or a philosophy. "Just the facts, ma'am" was hard. But at some point, I learned that everything is a story. And I didn't want to report stories. I wanted to write my own.

Journalism was excellent practice at the construction of writing. It also facilitated my learning to be concise. Notice I said *learning* to be concise. As in, "not yet mastered."

Stephen King said once that a writer must be willing to "kill your darlings, kill your darlings, even when it breaks your egocentric little scribbler's heart, kill your darlings."[1] As a student editor, I had no problem strangling another student's paragraph in the cradle, but I held on to my own sentences long enough to send them to college.

Faced with the inevitable second-phase education crisis of graduate school, I was torn between a master's in journalism and a law degree. Reasoning that I could always write without a master's, I decided on law school. I constructed a vision of myself as plaintiff's crusader. I would make justice happen. I would be a voice for the oppressed, dedicated to impugning the notion that might makes right. Also, I wanted to be smart and it seemed to me that law school was what smart people did.

It did not occur to me that there are 205 American Bar Association–approved law schools in the country, producing approximately forty thousand graduates each year. These numbers argue against the premise that all lawyers are smart. Some of them just have a proclivity for drudgery.

four

Buck Rogers

Some people, wise people, take a respite between life stages. They pause to reflect, to travel, to experience new things before shouldering the mantle of professional responsibility. I, on the other hand, have set numerous courses and plunged headlong without skipping a beat for so much as a nap. This is a function of my highly driven personality, and my need to just "get on with it." I have a problem being still. This is my mother's fault. My father once said her motor runs at a higher idle than most people's. Mine is in fifth gear all the time. Genetics, y'all.

Every summer in high school, I had a job. I started working in my father's law office when I was sixteen. My fifteen-year-old sister worked with me. "Worked" is to be interpreted in the loosest sense. I was plied with promises of Taco Bell at lunchtime. This was a prime example of how much I loved food (only slightly less than books) and also how easily manipulated I was. It took nothing more than a beef meximelt to get me off the couch. The work was simple enough: collating, stapling, mailing. Sometimes it involved taking Post-it notes off my back that said "kick me," lovingly placed there by my sister. I did some research in the local law library and inhaled the aroma of aged leather and old books.

My parents were industrious types, and even today, at an age at which they should be contemplating retirement, they travel more than a rock star on tour for the five jobs they hold between them. I am exhausted just *thinking* about the work they do. They likewise encouraged productivity in us. After that stint in my dad's office during high school, I joined him again as an intern when he became the regional director of a nonprofit civil rights firm.

This kind of work was headier stuff. I was now expected to do real work during my summers, with the understanding that what I was doing was contributing at least in some small degree to the exercise of First Amendment rights. The work involved lots of research and taught me the utility of caffeine when stuck ears-deep in research on constitutional standards of interpretation. But as nonprofits are wont, the association didn't pay its interns a salary. The experience was great, but I needed to bankroll something before law school started. Not realizing I would take home a sheepskin *and* $120,000 in student debt, I may as well have taken a month in Belize for all the good my next job was going to do. I had graduated from college a year early and had time to kill.

So, naturally, a job at the mall seemed like the perfect fit. Naturally.

Not wanting to leave books for long, I took a position at the Walden bookstore near my parents' home in Virginia.

Walden Books was a subsidiary of Borders at the time and expanded to include Coles Bookstores, WaldenKids, and Brentanos Books. There were at one point 205 retail locations in the United States. I mention this only to say that, after what seemed like a meteoric rise to bookstore predominance, the company was liquidated in bankruptcy in 2011, after I had worked for them. It is unnervingly coincidental. But probably unrelated, right?

At this point, I will say a little something about the fiefdom of retail stores. Particularly mall stores. Here is how the organization of people expresses the basest of human inclinations: everybody wants to be king. In our location, there were only eight employees. We were divided into managers, assistant managers, key holders, and proles. The proles held no power whatsoever. This meant that people like me—part-time, seasonal, temporary employees—could be dictated to by any eighteen-year-old key holder power tripping on telling us when we could take our lunch break. Key holders had the ability to open and close the store and to void transactions on the registers. They held no real power other than that indicated by the single key dangling from the red rubber bracelet on their skinny wrists. Assistant managers and managers had *real* key sets—janitorial-grade ensembles, heavy and brassy. They evoked real power. These were people who called headquarters to enter inventory data in the morning, counted money drawers at store open and close, and made deposits at the bank. I was just someone who loved books and was killing time.

Each of the proles and key holders was assigned an inventory section for which we were responsible. We stocked new books when they arrived and filled empty shelves when something sold down. We made regular passes through our assigned sections to straighten and maintain alphabetized order. Then we paced. And flipped through magazines. And made small talk. Our Walden Books location wasn't particularly big, and even with only three of us working in a day, there were more people than work. This meant I spent a lot of time falling more madly in love with books.

Which is a small miracle, as my assigned section was romance and I can't think of a genre I detest more.

If I saw one exposed bosom, I saw a peck, all on the same shelf. There was too much flowing hair and too many words like *abysmal* and *pusillanimous*, which were thrown around like *dark* and *shy* might be used by a normal person, and which are fine words in and of themselves but seem like a cheap way to up the ante when you're trying to fashion a one-hundred-thousand word count out of a paragraph's worth of plot. Also, there were only a few themes, recycled again and again with nothing more than different characters and different cover art. Romance novels came in one of five thematic varieties: (1) Renaissance, (2) Baroque, (3) high seas, (4) Revolutionary War, and (5) Civil War. There was an obvious lack of Great Depression tales, as if the writers didn't think there was some sweeping diorama of erotica to be explored in the dust bowl.

I wasn't banking enough hours to justify the hour-long round-trip to the mall every day, so I hunted around for a second retail job. I found one in the pinkest, most fragrant place on earth: Victoria's Secret.

I must provide some historical context here. When I worked at "Vicky's" (as the employees affectionately called it), there remained a separation between the fragrance and body shop, and the main lingerie and sleepwear store. A beautiful curved archway adorned with cherubs connected the two stores. I was hired immediately as a key holder in the fragrance shop (because these people recognized quality), and I was like a little girl let loose in an American Girl store. I got to spray, smell, and moisturize with everything that came in the front door. Delivery day was like Christmas. There were elaborate inventory and training manuals dedicated to the creation of the perfect upscale, luxurious environment. Vicky's was on the cusp of the trend of "affordable luxury." Yes, $12.50 seemed like a lot to spend on a hand cream. But because you *really* wanted to smell like iced pear, it was okay.

It must also be said that this was the Vicky's of twenty years ago. The Vicky's of twenty years ago sold classical music CDs along with French milled soaps and crystal atomizers of perfume. It sold satin mule slippers and closet sachets of lavender near satin padded hangers and silk robes. Its employees still knew what a trousseau was. This Vicky's was the last of a dying breed before it was replaced with its sluttier younger sister, who sells panties that don't really qualify as such because I'm sure they're missing some minimum fabric content. This Vicky spells her name with an "i," and her perfumes say *sex* right on the bottle. I tried to buy a set of plain cotton bikinis on my last trip into the store, and it took me ten minutes of untangling fishing wire to realize I'd gotten stuck in the G-strings. I actually had to ask someone which side the front was.

In the perfume department of Vicky's past, the room was lit from within with étagères of halogen light and glass. The floor was gleaming marble and there was an angelic façade behind the counter. We were to dress in heels and skirts and avoid garish makeup or jewelry. I loved it so much I eventually quit my bookstore job to continue my romance with luxury. I spent hours with Windex and a towel cleaning smudges from glass shelving. I wiped the tester bottles down and straightened signs. I greeted people. I chatted with them about their purchases. Willingly.

I made fast friends with a woman named Nancy who, like me, was biding her time before law school. She was headed to the University of Delaware and, also like me, had graduated with an odd gap between undergraduate and graduate school. There was also Barb, who was misplaced but one of the nicest women I've met. She'd come from a security job at Best Buy and was brought in to eliminate "shrink," which is the nice word people in the retail industry have for a woman who stuffs five bras in her purse when she thinks you're not looking. Barb had been hired specifically because she was both a woman and tough, but she happened to be one of the kindest people I'd ever met. She also seemed genuinely happy to finally get a chance to work with other women. When the stores in our district competed for sales goals during particular promotional periods, Barb would bring in poster board signs she'd written with a Sharpie at home. They'd say things like, "C'mon, girls! Let's take the money and run!" I remember this sign because it was so cute and yet so misguided. It sounded like she was encouraging our criminal behavior and none of us were old enough to realize that "Take the Money and Run" was a song by the Steve Miller Band, so the effect was lost.

Then there was my friend Tatiana. She was a Ukrainian transplant by way of Canada and spoke with a combination of confidence and hypnosis that made her numbers skyrocket.

If the accent didn't close the sale, then her bold bangles and mile-long legs did. She could have been Vicky's poster girl. I thought she hung the moon. Particularly because she had an adorable manner of ending every statement like a question. "Because we are closing the sale, yes?" Every time I saw our names on the work schedule together, I did a happy golf clap. Working with Tatiana was like going to hang out with one of your best friends in your favorite store. Let me rephrase: it wasn't *like* that, it actually *was* that. Life was good. Until the Christmas shopping season started.

I tip my hat to you, holiday retail workers. I am pretty sure that when Dante wrote the *Divine Comedy*, he was using "mall during Christmastime" as his vision for hell's seventh level. There is something about the combination of desperation, debt, and fatigue that makes it nearly unbearable. It all stinks, because the beautiful, pure, and simplistic meaning of Christmas is often lost in the melee of consumerism. And I was about to get an up close and personal experience with consumerism. No longer was I the eight-year-old in pigtails wishing for a Barbie car on Christmas morning as I tiptoed down in my pink footie pajamas. Now I was just one bottle of perfume away from an angry mob.

The first Christmas was the worst. I have a high tolerance for travail, so a twelve-hour shift on my feet seemed a great way to double my income. Never having worked a retail outlet during the holiday season, however, I had no idea what I was in for. Plus, I was doing it in heels and pantyhose. My feet have never recovered. I have a little toe that became permanently stuck in a state of forty-five-degree angle flexion. This was bad news for my collection of totally impractical shoes.

I pulled into the mall parking lot the day after Thanksgiving, and there was a line already starting outside the glass front doors. A gaggle of women stood there with their teeny weeny knapsacks and their coffees. Some carried their own shopping bags. I was mystified. I had barely been able to drag myself out of bed after injecting my body with the tryptophan of a huge turkey dinner the night before, and these people were raring to buy something they could just as easily buy a few hours later.

It was about ten in the morning when the trouble started. By this time the first earlybird shoppers had dispatched and the rest of northern Virginia was waking up from under their gravy blankets to come pouring in the front doors. As a mini-manager in the perfume shop, I was accomplishing plenty on my own, but at one point the register jammed. Through the curved door in the clothing department, they were wrapping undies in pink tissue faster than sub sandwiches at a deli. But at least their registers were working. It just so happened that my register jammed at a moment when a short woman with dark hair and a scowl came up to my counter with two bottles of lotion. She exhaled deeply as I tried in vain to get the machine up and running again. The sighs became louder. I looked up at her.

"I'm so sorry about this. I should be able to help you over on the other side of the store."

I motioned for her to accompany me to the back registers and then extended my hand to the shorter of the two lincs. I then told Tatiana my register had jammed and while I waited for the fix, would she be so kind as to ring this woman up? Tatiana looked up and smiled to the woman.

"Absolutely. I will ring you up in one minute, yes?"

Then I returned to the perfume shop to fight with the machine. Which is when I heard a voice behind me.

"Uh, excuse me? I thought you said you could help me on the other side of the store!"

I turned to face the squat woman with the lotion bottles and flushed fifty shades of red.

"Well, ma'am, I'm so sorry but you have to wait until one of the registers opens. There are lines—"

"This is ridiculous!" she screeched at me. "You told me you were going to take care of me, and you didn't! I'm going to get the manager!"

As someone who is totally, completely, deeply averse to conflict, I was practically sick. I wracked my brain for what I could have done differently. Barb came around the corner to speak to the angry troll, who proceeded to relay the story to her and everyone within earshot with increasing volume. Customers came around the corner from the store's opposite side to gawk. I'm sure they were thinking a fight in a Victoria's Secret was going to be loads of fun. Who would throw the first bra?

Barb looked at me and asked for my version of the story. My version was exactly the same as the customer's, except it was given with downcast eyes. I suddenly felt guilty but couldn't figure out what I'd done wrong. Barb then asked the dark-haired woman what she could do to right the perceived wrong.

In retail, the mantra goes, "The customer is always right." The employees of Victoria's Secret were given training manuals instructing us to do whatever was necessary to placate the patrons of the store. We were to accept their word as gospel. Unless, of course, they were caught stuffing pajamas in their oversized purses. And even then, it practically necessitated security footage. There were myriad ways to get around the "rules" of store operations and get something for nothing at our store. I had to handle returns of things that were *clearly worn*. Worn many, many times. The only time we turned merchandise away was when the tag read something like "Hanes," proving it wasn't even something we sold. I'm surprised no one tried to return a car battery. This is how customer-favored our operations were.

So when Barb asked this woman what it was she wanted as recompense, it took her no time at all to respond. "I want you to fire her."

She wanted me fired because she had to wait an extra five minutes to buy some lotion. I looked at Barb with eyes that may have been the teeniest bit glassy from threatening tears.

Barb took a deep breath, and in a voice that came somewhere from the depths of her six-foot frame, responded, "Not only will I not fire her, she was recently promoted. The best I'm going to do is give you 50 percent off your purchase. I'll also take your name and address and see if corporate wants to do anything else for you." I wanted to jump into Barb's arms and thank her for protecting me. I would have done it, too, if I thought I could have jumped that high.

As it turned out, corporate decided that I had to issue a formal apology to the customer by way of a letter on Victoria's Secret stationary. After much deliberation on the appropriate wording, I penned the following:

Dear Ms. X:

I am very sorry that you had a bad experience when visiting our store on November 27th. When and if you should visit our store again, please don't hesitate to call on me for anything you might need.

Signed,
Sarah Parshall

I spritzed the letter with some of the store's signature perfume and dropped it in the mailbox outside the mall.

Thus ended my brief and ignominious retail career.

five

Res Ipsa . . . What'd You Say?

There's nothing like a little Latin to get a party started.

That's a lie. Latin basically turns everybody off unless you're a lawyer or a classics major, though it does make for a sometimes-welcome party trick. Matt, God love him, used to tell people that his girlfriend "spoke Latin" when we started going out. But you can't really have a conversation with someone in an ancient language when all you know how to say are things like "produce the body" or "buyer beware."

Law school was harder than I had conceived but also very rewarding. I would love to be a professional student. I love to read and write and research. I like the tidiness of producing things for a grade. I like the digestibility of projects with start and end dates. Book manuscripts are like this, but during the period in which you are supposed to be writing it is very

51

easy to be distracted by everything else going on around you. Not in the beginning, though. In the beginning, the deadline always seems *so* far in the future, and you are not threatened by the potential of the outside world hosing your plans until you start to close in on a date on the calendar. Then things like your son being home sick from school and interrupting you every nine minutes for a snack can make you want to throw your laptop across the room.

Before the books I was writing came the books I was reading.

Practicing law was nowhere near as fun as studying law. Though most nights I had to squeeze my eyelids open in attempts to stay awake during such adventures as an examination of whether deadly force was permissible in defending an uninhabited property, my sizeable collection of legal texts was a source of (misplaced) pride. Buying the same $126 textbook as all your classmates is not a thing distinguishable. I liked the heaviness of the books, their apparent importance. I loved setting them up in my apartment during graduate school, and later in my new office with a view of downtown. I loved their look, spread open on my desk. The books were part of what I finally thought I'd developed: a sense of worth based on my vocation. The denser they were, the thicker they were, the better. I displayed my books in the same way people sometimes carry around unopened versions of David Foster Wallace's *Infinite Jest* to prove they know it's a thing. A thing smart people know. A thing not a lot of people actually read.

For me, the brain was the thing. Even after high school, where I hadn't been prom queen or cheerleading captain but had taken calculus for "fun." Where I had been voted "most likely to become president," which wasn't so much a function of intellect but maybe more a consequence of being too opinionated.

I wanted smarts so bad that I thought stuffing my head full of information could make up for any intellectual deficiency. Law school sounds boring to a lot of people, because for a lot of people it is. But I cared so much about the imbued pride I got from saying I was a lawyer that I'd supplanted the concept of an actual "calling." What did God actually desire for me to do? I knew I wanted to help people. That was a given. But every service performed or good provided is an attempt to "help" people. You "help" people clear their lawns by selling leaf blowers at Home Depot. You "help" people smell better by stocking deodorant at CVS.

I'm able to look back now and realize in how many contexts I've used my degree. It's come in handy, for certain. But comparatively, among all its other uses, I've used my law degree the least in a "traditional context"—as in the actual practice of law. I didn't understand it then, but when the designation started to lose its luster I likewise started to lose interest in what I was doing.

Things started out great. In fact, if I'd stuck with the first part of my legal work, I might still be in it. Our Baltimore-based firm was one of a few in the city with a specialty in admiralty and maritime law. This practice area involves the representation of everyone who might in any way be connected to work performed on or near a ship. It can involve shipowners, the owners of the containers on the ship, the workers on the ship, or the workers on the dock who unload the ship. If a product is moved from one place to another by waterway, at some point our firm had probably been involved.

I had a hand in international commerce. (Fine. A pinky.) That was something, wasn't it?

My grandfather was a naval captain. John Paul Jones, father of the American Navy, is an ancestor. I spent my teenage summers at a lake and spend my adult summers at the ocean. My innards are more water than blood. Here, I thought, was something that fit. Maritime law was smart and cool, and I was interested in it—and people were interested in me because I did it. When I hung out with my other lawyer friends, the suckers stuck doing tax law and corporate mergers, I would coolly tell them I had arrested a ship that day.

So, yeah, basically I was Catwoman.

Our offices were a few blocks from the federal courthouse, where we would file maritime liens and the associated requests for arrest. Arresting ships is super fun. Once you get over your sheer terror at marching up the gangplank behind a federal marshal while a bunch of crew members glower at you and curse at you in Croatian, it's a real trip. Under the Federal Maritime Lien Act, if a shipowner fails to pay its crew or provide necessary accommodations, and attempts at resolution have failed, you can literally duct tape an arrest warrant to the steering wheel and the ship has to stay in port until things are resolved. Which is why the Croatian crew is glowering at you. Because now they're stuck in a city where no one knows how to take an order for a cheeseburger in Croatian.

My legal work was a combination of smart and tough. And my mental fantasies abounded. They included (1) me, marching up the stairs of the federal courthouse and pushing reporters out of the way as I fought my way in to file super important paperwork; (2) me, slamming my fist on counsel's table in front of the old-guard judge who wasn't going to listen to the plaintiff's case, certainly not one argued by a woman; and (3) me, hugging my client as the verdict was read in our favor and later buying everyone drinks as we toasted our victory under the stars.

Half of my legal career was fantasy, come to think of it. I realize now that law was an unconscious way to create an exterior shell to protect my jellyfish insides, a part of me that I felt was weak and ignorant and easily injured. I thought saying I was a lawyer would somehow both impress others and protect me at the same time.

The Falinski sisters cracked that shell right open.

Maritime work was only a portion of our firm's focus. Much of it centered on the day-to-day commercial litigation that powers most small firms: things like contract disputes, landlord grievances, employment discrimination claims, and real estate cases. The higher-profile, higher-dollar cases went, as they ought, to the partners whose billable rates were twice mine. That meant that I got the remainders, the smaller cases. I learned there was an inverse relationship between the monetary value of a case and how often the clients will call you to ask about said case. In other words, a five-thousand-dollar dispute means you will get approximately ten thousand calls in the course of a week. A million-dollar case means you will get exactly one.

In a small, residential portion of eastern Baltimore, the Falinski sisters had held to a decades-old zoning variance that allowed them to operate a bar called Tony's Place. It bore nothing more than a small neon sign the size of a bread box and a parking lot big enough for only three cars.

The parking lot was the crux of the Falinskis' lawsuit: they were staking a claim to approximately twelve lost feet of parking space. The neighbor had a troublesome habit of parking his small boat on the left side of his house, which shared a common boundary with the parking lot at Tony's Place. The Falinski sisters wanted to sue on the basis of that disputed boundary line, stating that the loss of this space was sending at least one paying customer away because there was nowhere for said potential customer to park. The Falinski sisters were good of heart but bloody of tooth, and they were out to drive their neighbor from his home, taking his boat and his sense of entitlement with him.

Each day calls from the Falinski sisters rolled in. The younger sister, eager to please her older and more cantankerous sibling, called me every day. Sometimes twice a day. I grew to dread the buzz of my desk phone. "These things take time," I would tell her. "Opposing counsel still has ten days to answer our motion," I would explain. But every day she called hoping that the neighbor had given up, decided to sell his house, and given the sisters the entirety of his proceeds as damages for lost business at Tony's Place. To make it worse, the neighbor and defendant in our case was dying of cancer. His wife was overwhelmed with his treatments and her attempts to protect their own flagging business, and now she had to deal with two sisters who were out to claim twelve feet of pavement. It was hard for me to even face the defendant's wife in the hallway during our hearings. I just wanted to put my arms around her and tell her I was sorry about the whole thing. (By the way, you cannot do this when you're a lawyer. I guess it's considered bad form.)

The judge denied our motion for summary judgment—a way to determine the case and issue a ruling before the parties get to trial. I told the Falinskis that there was a good chance we would lose at trial and that prior settlement would give them enough money to repave the parking lot and provide additional space. I told them how expensive continued litigation would be—all to no avail.

Walking the younger sister to her car after a client meeting one day, I explained what my next steps would be based on our discussions. She interrupted me.

"Wait—are you a lawyer? I thought you were a paralegal, hon."

I blinked at her so many times I'm sure it looked like I'd been maced.

"No," I replied cautiously. "Only a lawyer can file motions, appear in court, depose witnesses. You know. The things I've been doing for you for six months?"

I thought suddenly of the first motion I'd ever been called to defend, at the ripe old age of twenty-five. I thought of what the judge had said when I appeared at the counsel table and the way he looked down the bridge of his aquiline nose from a desk that seemed forty feet in the air. "Young lady, is there anyone else coming that's going to be defending the motion today? Or is it just you?"

From the start, it was as if the world didn't believe I was a lawyer. Notwithstanding the fact that I am cooler than any lawyer living or dead, I began having trouble believing I was a lawyer, too. Outside the SunTrust Insurance building, I waved Ms. Falinski off as she headed to her car, and thought to myself, *What am I doing here?* I had wanted two things: to help people solve problems and to totally impress people with my super fly career. I was failing at both.

The time for navel gazing and plan making became available when I contracted mononucleosis a month later and had to take an extended leave of absence from the firm. When I returned, I quit my job cold turkey without another prospect in sight. This was highly uncharacteristic of me. It was also highly risky, because I was paying enough in student debt each month to buy my own very nice boat and park it on someone else's parking lot.

I flipped through papers on the couch as I recovered, stabbing at any job that caught my attention and thinking foolishly that a law degree made me qualified to do anything.

It didn't.

I halfheartedly applied to other law firms, but no one was hiring. I made it to second and third interview rounds and received every assurance that an offer would come, only to be told later that the firm had decided to increase their lawyer's required hours to cover the work rather than make an outside hire. I suppose there was some small part of me that was glad, because if these schlubs were already billing fifty hours a week and now had to bill sixty, I guessed they were going to be pretty miserable. Matt asked me what I thought I might want to do. I found myself at a crossroads. A weird one. I had these degrees, but I had shifted course and was not even sure how I would use them.

My parents must have sensed my growing discontent, because that Christmas they bought me two books: one titled *The Lawyer's Calling* and the other called *Running from the Law*. Like they were hoping I might continue to practice but had a sneaking suspicion I was one foot out the door.

A few weeks later, I found a local paper with a list of the city's best advertising agencies.

Huh. Advertising, I thought. *That sounds interesting.*

And just like that, my career path and my work took another abrupt turn.

six

Madison Avenue Madness

I blame *Mad Men* for making advertising look as entertaining as Perry Mason once did for the law. I'm sure it's to blame for at least 50 percent of the advertising careers in the United States. I also blame Donny Deutsch of the massive advertising firm Deutsch, Inc. for his recurring presence on every major television outlet. In much the same way that I once thought a law degree made me qualified to do anything, Donny thinks an advertising career makes him qualified to *talk* about anything. It's misleading. Unless you're in school working toward a marketing degree and hoping to run your own agency someday. Then it's the flag you plant and work toward until you get tired of writing copy for fertilizer ads. Only 0.002 percent of ad executives work on accounts such as Coke or Delta Airlines. The rest just write jingles for the local plumbing guy.

What qualifications did I possess to pursue a career in advertising? The answer is zero. Exactly zero qualifications. But I sent résumés to every agency in town. I did know enough about marketing to understand that agencies are divided into the "creative" brains and the "business" brains. The partners—the good ones—possess both. As a lawyer, I knew no one was going to hire me as a graphic designer or a media buyer, but I might be of some benefit to the business brains.

After a series of emphatic "nos" (many of which involved statements like, "There's no possible way we'd be able to afford you," which was too bad, because they'd clearly overestimated how much I'd been making), I got one last phone call. The Gresham Group was a Baltimore-based agency that employed about forty people and specialized in travel and tourism marketing. They'd handled the Puerto Rico Convention and Visitor's Bureau account, as well as tourism for the city of Baltimore itself. But their sales were flagging. They needed someone to drive business and pitch new accounts. The partner asked me a few questions over the phone, and I must have passed muster, because the next week I went to the city for an in-person interview.

Walking the halls, I realized just how colorful was the rabbit hole into which I'd fallen. For as plain and tan and unified as the law firm was, the advertising agency was its exact opposite, a kaleidoscope of creative talent, and every corner reflected it. Pictures, posters, and photography hung from the walls. There were figurines and bobbling trinkets on desktops. There were things that glowed and things that lit up, and I was introduced to that mysterious, colorful creature—the Macintosh computer. I'm told people call these "Macs," but I haven't wanted to exhibit infidelity to the PC that's seen me through three books, so I don't much care. Except for the fact that Matt has an "air Mac" that weighs less than a can of soup and is paper-thin and blessedly convenient. This annoys me slightly because it's the newest possible technology and it's something to which I feel entitled, as a relative "creative" type. I've been indoctrinated by too much television showing writers on Macs. I've rejected them mainly because I am impatient; I don't have the desire to learn new technology while trying to actually get my job done. At the Gresham Group I was asked by the technology manager which type of computer I wanted. I asked for a PC, and I could hear the laughter all the way down the hallway.

Three partners ran the agency, but the accounting partner had left the hiring of a business development director (me) to the purview of the two chief creative officers who were the agency's other two partners. They also happened to be married to one another. I'm not sure how anything got done with a leadership team of three people, two of whom happened to be married. Also, because my office was going to be in the heart of the lyrical, electric place where ideas were birthed to the tune of the Foo Fighters playing on the ad director's computer, I did get a chance to see them fight about things like whose turn it was to pick up their daughter from daycare. My desk was right across from both partners' glass-front offices. I still hated conflict. Now I had a front-row seat.

I did love my creative co-workers though. And I think they were at least marginally entertained by me, the weird quasi-bookish type who used to work at something called a "law firm." After a few months, my copywriter friend Susan did tell me, "We were pretty sure you were too cool to be an actual lawyer." Which is about the highest praise you can get when you're a lawyer in an ad agency—a workplace practically synonymous with "cool people." I worked with a talented group who saw the world in a way I'd never considered. We once pitched the State of Maryland tourism account and turned the entirety of the office into an American picnic scene with checkered blankets, beach balls, children playing, and somebody's golden retriever. We held another event to thank our current clients and highlight our travel and tourism expertise, and for this we converted the entire office into a tour of the world, with different departments playing the role of different nations—from Puerto Rico to Africa. My friend Susan, my art director friend Julie, and I turned the art department into Russia. From a great, white, stuffed bear, to Russian drinking songs, to a smoke machine and cotton "snow drifts," I was fairly certain I had landed the greatest job in the world. Particularly when we got some new business out of the event I'd had a hand in planning and I came out looking like a rock star.

I proved to be braver on the phone than I was in person. I once pitched our agency to FedEx. *FedEx.* I mean, for the love! Like they were just going to ditch their current billion-dollar agency in favor of a regional agency that was relatively unknown for no good reason other than the fact that the young lady on the phone seemed like a nice enough gal. I did lead the charge on writing our response to the requests for proposals that led to the new accounts, though. And I either wrote or edited the contracts and licenses that developed as a result of business we had won. On slower days, some of the copywriters even let me brainstorm campaign ideas with them.

Brainstorming is that thing where one copywriter lies on a couch and throws a tennis ball at the ceiling while another one leans back at his desk with a pencil in his teeth and his hands clasped behind his head. It does not in any way resemble work, but it is fabulous in that you can't really mess up, and the concept is to develop a volume of material and sort the good from the bad after everything is on the table. What I do now doesn't look much like work either. Just ask my children. When I lift my hands from the keyboard for so much as thirty seconds, they think I'm "done," and they swarm me like angry hornets. I have resorted to typing things like "asldkjf wpowo0v mnaodklh" just to keep my fingers moving so they'll leave me alone.

At the ad agency, I was the token square in an office full of ovals—kind of a reverse affirmative action hire. But I loved my new work family. And it was perfect. Mostly.

Everyone at the agency had fabulous pictures on their walls, rock group posters, and pop art. I had nothing to hang on my walls. Nothing funny or artistic or cute. I had boring licenses and framed diplomas. But they were all I had, so I hung them. My undergraduate degree is from Liberty University in Lynchburg, Virginia. It's the school founded years ago by Reverend Jerry Falwell. Yes, *the* Jerry Falwell.

The married partners—the ones across from whose offices I worked, and to whom I answered—were rather left of center. And when I say "left," imagine a baseball field. Now imagine the third baseline. Now imagine the nosebleed bleacher seats directly to the left of the left field third baseline. *That* left of center. They were self-professed agnostics who supported causes that were the opposite of things I held to be true. This did not prove problematic to me in any way.

Nor was it an impediment to my getting my work done and done well.

It was an impediment for one of the partners, though.

He would come in and chat every so often about what kind of accounts he would like to land and our plan for upcoming meetings. We had a great rapport. Until he looked above my desk one day.

Midsentence, the partner broke cadence as he looked at my diplomas. He asked if I had graduated from *the* Liberty University, the one of famed televangelist association, the Christian school he'd heard of, the one he particularly despised.

I told him it was the very same university.

Then he said, "I can't believe you went to that fascist school! How did you get in here?" The blood rose in his face.

Then he stood up and pivoted on his heel, walking right into his wife's office across the hall. The door slammed behind him.

I picked up my purse and, with as much forced nonchalance as I could muster, I took the elevator down to the parking garage. After climbing the outside ramp on shaking legs, I reached my parked car and dialed my husband.

"Matt, I think they are going to fire me," I cried. My hands were trembling. He asked what had happened. Had I been embezzling? Was I mooning the account executives? Stealing office supplies?

I relayed the story of what had happened, and he chuckled. "You know they can't fire you for that, right?"

He was right in that they couldn't fire me because of my religious affiliation, but never in a written record would it appear that they had decided to terminate me because of my beliefs. Oh no. They had better sense than that. Most employers do. But that wasn't to say they wouldn't let me go because they were "downsizing" or had decided the position was "unnecessary" or some other trumped-up phrasing. I was an at-will employee. This was the default employer-employee relationship in the state of Maryland where I was working, and it meant that unless there existed an express contract between both parties, an individual could be terminated for any reason so long as it was not "illegal," i.e., discriminatory.

More than anything, I was just mystified that I had been so liked one minute and so reviled the next. The speed of this change of heart had been terrifying, and I found it so irrelevant to doing my job that it was heartbreaking. Take a type A personality and tell her that she's failing, but don't tell her the formula for success, and you're sure to drive her mad.

I wasn't about to quit, that was for sure. And if they were going to fire me for what I believed, then the Lord had willed it so. This had been the only advertising agency in town to give me a job. I could have ended up anywhere, but God had opened this door. For this moment. For a reason.

With a deep breath, I walked back through the garage and into the office, holding my head high as I made my way down the hall. I sat back down at my desk. A few minutes later, my boss came in to stammer through a halfhearted apology. He said something about being sorry for calling it a fascist school, along with other words vaguely related and barely audible. Because his wife had a decent head on her shoulders, I'm certain she'd told him to apologize because none of the partners wanted a discrimination lawsuit on their hands. Ironically, the lawyer he had hired—me—was the least litigious person he would ever meet. I didn't even like getting paid to sue people, let alone sue them just to make a point. But I didn't miss an opportunity to give him some good-natured ribbing before he left my office.

"You know, I thought you liberals were supposed to be the open-minded ones."

He laughed. A genuine from-the-gut laugh. And I told him I hoped he would be pleasantly surprised by me, that it was good for him to work side by side with someone he might have disliked had he met her at a party. I clearly had enough of a brain in my head to have been hired. And his executive assistant had told me a few days prior, during one of our new business pitches, that she couldn't remember the last time there was so much business coming through the door.

I am not a creature of revenge. I am, however, a creature of tireless commitment to things toward which I aim. I "work hard so [I] can present [myself] to God and receive his approval. [I strive to] be a good worker, one who does not need to be ashamed" (2 Tim. 2:15 NLT). I wasn't working for the agency, really. The partner didn't know that. All he knew was that I was reliable and dedicated. All he knew was that the first Christian with whom he'd ever worked was contradicting his preconceptions in little, wonderful ways.

seven

The Teacher Is In

After a while, the agnostic and the Christian went back to working side by side. I was happy to prove to him that I didn't have an extra ear or pray nightly to a lamp. We had an excellent relationship, and together we added meetings and sales pitches to the agency's roster of commitments. There were more client parties and budding opportunities. I got to listen in on new radio spots and weigh in on billboards and logos. But the ink was still wet on those new client contracts when I started to get restless again. Something was still missing. I thought it might be time to try another avenue. There were holes in my life I was angling to fill.

I subscribed to an email list that inventoried open positions for schools and colleges to teach in the fields of journalism, pre-law, and marketing. I think at one point I even threw English in there as an option. (Please forgive me, my English professor friends. I was young and immature.) I figured if I couldn't be a career student, maybe I could teach students as a supplemental career. I wasn't looking to leave the agency. Just experiment on the side. Just plug the giant crater in my self-worth. My boss ok'd this pursuit, as long as it didn't interfere with my work at the agency.

Notwithstanding the fact that I am usually just one Xanax shy of a total breakdown when I get up in front of a crowd, I get really jazzed up about the exchange of ideas and the discovery of things. I had loved school. Tapping into that passion seemed a perfect match. But I didn't have a degree in education. Like just about everything in my life, I took the germ of an idea and jumped in headfirst. I have friends who are about 570 times smarter than me who actually teach—and have multiple advanced degrees. I realize that this indifference to the qualifications needed for college-level teaching was maybe a tad ridiculous on my part. I blame it on not knowing any better at the time. I also blame it on the fact that I was on a pilgrimage for some kind of valuation I had yet to find. Desperation for a sought thing can make someone inflate their capabilities to get it. I was looking to peg myself somewhere, and I hadn't yet found the place that fit. I was on some kind of a career vision quest without the peyote. *Hey, I figured out how to work in advertising, so . . . why can't I teach a college class?*

You know. Naturally.

I found an ad through Monster.com that told me Baltimore County Community College was seeking adjunct professors for business classes. One in particular caught my eye. It was an opening for a teacher of business ethics (Management 265), a requisite class for anyone pursuing a business degree. Advanced degrees in the field of law or philosophy were preferred, as was real-world business experience. I zipped off a résumé and a cover letter that explained why I would be a good fit, and I got a call the very next day to come in for an interview.

When I arrived at the campus in Catonsville, I felt a little vibration of excitement. I was going to carry textbooks. I would be called "Mrs. Perry." I found the office of Paul Sanders, the chair of the business department, and introduced myself. Paul was a heavyset man with thick glasses and a tumbleweed of white hair folded over a mostly bald scalp. His office was that of a man in the clutches of disorganized overwork. To say he "interviewed" me might be an embellishment of what transpired. It was essentially an instant job offer with some small talk mixed in to enhance the appearance of the licit. It benefited us both, actually. I left with a sample course outline and a few old texts, thinking I was big noise. He probably high-fived everyone down the hall because he'd unloaded a class that, I learned at a later date, was nearly impossible to fill. Business ethics was the curricular dog, and I had just been handed the leash. All business students had to take it. None of the professors wanted to teach it.

As this was a once-a-week class, it fell to me to fill two whole hours of class time. Assuming a ten minute bathroom/snack/cellphone break, that is still an infernally long block of time to fill when one has no experience teaching and has only general familiarity with the course material. There was some overlap with case law I'd studied in law school, but once we got into material on environmental policy or the FDA's history of tobacco regulation, I started hitting the books harder than my students (you know, assuming they were hitting them at all). The class was a "breakfast club" cliché, replete with jocks, princesses, and dark, brooding eccentrics. On a good day, three of fifteen students were actually taking notes. The rest were either texting or napping. It did not at any point dawn on me to tell these students to pay attention. I had not yet fully realized I was in charge. I was not a distinguished academic with multiple papers published on the subject matter of my course, one who'd gone to school with the understanding that she'd one day be standing in front of an audience and advocating open minds. No. I was an insecure working girl staring at a field of unimpressed faces and on my way to being downright heckled for a measly $250 a month.

The first day, I walked into class with a quaking gut and a huge bottle of water to address the desert-grade dry mouth I was experiencing. I was suddenly overcome by the completely reasonable fear of being exposed as a fraud. At twenty-eight, I wasn't much older than some of the students in my class. For one particular student I was much younger, and this proved to be a problem.

His name was Abram. An observant Jew, he wore prayer locks and a prayer shawl under his black coat. He took a seat in the center of the room and stared at me while I removed books and outlines from my briefcase. Like he couldn't figure out what kind of strange new species I was. I could feel his eyes like a laser on the back of my head. I introduced myself to the room and gave some information on my background. But here is the problem with background information when you're twenty-eight: there isn't much of it. It's a real short list of accomplishments. Abram wasn't about to let that go unnoticed.

I was ready to move into the first lesson when Abram yelled out, "You're pretty young, aren't you? Did you practice in ethics?"

I steadied myself on the podium.

"Well, one doesn't 'practice' in the area of ethics. Ethics are a mode of dealing in business. I've done work in civil rights and—"

"What kind of work?" he shot back, itching for a fight.

"I litigated a Title VII lawsuit against a pharmaceutical—"

Not quitting. Not slowing down at all. Not getting quieter, even.

"But now you're in advertising?"

I don't know why it surprised me that someone was calling my academic credibility into question. I just knew that I had to shut this thing down before the whole class devolved into chaos and students started throwing books at me like agitated monkeys.

I was an adjunct, for Pete's sake. Didn't he understand I had a different full-time job during the day?

"Abram," I choked, "I'd like to get into the first lesson, please."

This was the first step in a pattern that lasted the entire semester. Every Tuesday night from 6 to 8 p.m., I had to defend myself against a student who had a compulsive need to shout out his contradictions to every statement I made. I came home exhausted, wailing to Matt that it was hard enough standing up in front of class and teaching for nearly two hours without feeling like I was in front of a firing squad. Couldn't they just slavishly accept what I was saying as gospel, like I had done with my own professors?

Finally, eight weeks into the class, Abram blurted something out about how I had misinterpreted the court's ruling in *Farris v. Glen Alden Corporation* relative to de facto corporate mergers, and I very nearly lost my mind. I was over the initial fear of teaching the material, and knowing just how much time I had spent prepping for the lesson (answer: too much, even for a constitutional law class at an Ivy League school), I knew I had it right. The other students had started groaning with the launch of his newest diatribe, so I also knew I had the weight of popular opinion behind me. This helped me pull up my big girl pants and hold up my hand to interrupt him.

"Excuse me, Abram. I believe only one of us is teaching this class. If you have something to say, you may see me after class to share your thoughts. I'm going to ask you to leave if you interrupt me again."

The class burst into applause.

Abram was mute until the end of the semester. For their final grade, each student had to take one of the cases we'd studied during the semester and make a comparison to a current news story involving the issue of business ethics. They could choose from governmental regulation of business, mergers and acquisitions, the law of agency, or the nature of the corporation. Each presentation was to be five minutes and would be followed by a Q&A period. I was fairly pleased with myself until I realized this assignment required me to set about sixty-two Google alerts so I'd have an actual comparative basis against which to set the grading curve. I had to know what on earth was going on in the world of business ethics on all of these topics so I didn't look like an idiot.

Some of the students went all-out, and my heart nearly exploded with pride. They had listened! They had taken the assignment seriously! They made presentation notes! Some even had PowerPoints, and some handed out copies of articles from publications.

The students presented in alphabetical order. By virtue of his last name, Abram was last. When he got up in front of the class, it was obvious he was winging it. He didn't bring up so much as a Post-it note. Could it be that Abram had used up all his rhetoric during the course of the semester, and so had very little to say? I asked him a question at the end of his "presentation," and after scrambling to answer, he turned to me.

"Well, what do you think?"

Oh, *now* he wanted to listen to me.

After grading all the projects and turning in the materials to Paul at the end of the semester, he handed me a stack of evaluations in return.

With the kind of trepidation that I imagine precedes base jumping, I opened the stack. The evaluations were all positive, glowing even.

And then there was Abram's, which said simply: "Best class I took this semester."

People never cease to surprise me. I am always blindsided by their unexpected goodness.

Paul sent me an email a week after my grades were in, asking if I would be interested in teaching Management 265 again next semester, and maybe another class in addition to it. I told him that while I would love to, the classwork had proven too time consuming for me. I told him to keep me in mind for future classes. But in my heart, I knew I was done with teaching.

The next time I taught, it was going to be with people who were even louder, more disruptive, and certainly more surprising than Abram ever was.

Like Abram, however, they would constantly be questioning my authority.

• • • • •

At this point in my life, I had bounced from career to career and from degree to degree for years. I'd fabricated some checkered form of a work history based on the answer to a simple question: "What do you do for a living?" I'd taken full advantage of the freedom to change course with the wind. But I'd also discovered something disconcerting: difficulty gave me an excuse to run. So did frustration. And monotony. So a funny thing happened on the way to growing up. I became a mom, and I entered the profession of parenthood in which difficulty, frustration, and monotony are the official uniform. I couldn't pinball anymore. I couldn't run from difficult people. There wasn't a paycheck or a title to incite my performance.

And I couldn't ever quit.

Do These Children Come with Dental?

Each man's work shall be made manifest: for the day
shall declare it.

1 Corinthians 3:13 (ASV)

The phrase "working mother" is redundant.

Jane Sellman

eight

The Weirdos
Next Door

March 20, 1999

Our heroine opens her eyes to the Backstreet Boys playing on
the clock radio beside her bed. The light is already stream-
ing in through the large windows of her garden apartment,
and she shuffles into the kitchen for a cup of coffee before
picking out a skirt, a baby pink sweater, and kitten heels
from her walk-in closet. She showers and takes her time
doing her makeup and curling her hair, making use of the
abundant space in her bathroom and the second sink she
barely uses. Once ready, she reaches for her coat and grabs a
book from her bookcase. It is Haldor Laxness's *Independent
People*. The book will accompany her on the subway ride
downtown, where she is free to read and think with similarly
reticent passengers headed into the city for their workdays.

Not talking energizes her for the day ahead. She finds the quietude mentally productive.

She is the subway's last stop, at Charles Street Station. She walks up the staircase and into the light of the Baltimore morning. The time is 8:32 a.m. Her path takes her past street vendors, a florist, and a Greek restaurant from which she will later buy a gyro for lunch. She reaches the SunTrust building and takes the elevator to the fourth floor. Once inside the office, she greets the receptionist, who is also one of her closest friends. They chat for a few minutes before our heroine makes her way to her office, unpacks, and finds the managing partner to discuss the day's work. A motion needs to be filed, and there is a deposition scheduled in the conference room for later in the afternoon. She will take a break at lunch to do some online shopping, perusing for shoes and some cosmetics, and will later catch up with one of the paralegals over coffee. In all, she will bill eight hours of work today and meticulously enter her efforts into the office's timesheet program. As her workday draws to a close, she takes one last glance over her shoulder at her spotless office and then turns off the light.

Back outside, the street is cast in pink by the setting sun. Our heroine stops to pick up a bunch of flowers from a street merchant and takes them with her on her subway ride home, where she returns to her book and a calendar in which she makes notes for the coming weeks. At her apartment, she cooks herself an Asian stir-fry with ginger, garlic, and water chestnuts. She eats it on the couch while watching *Ally McBeal*, musing that it's great someone finally made a show about lawyers that's interesting. Her Himalayan cat makes itself a nuisance as she tidies the kitchen and rummages for a snack from some organic treats in the freezer. Then she calls a friend and makes plans for dinner and dancing for the weekend.

At 11:45, she retires for the night to a spacious bedroom that smells of the flowers on her nightstand. The ones she remembered to pick up on her way home.

March 20, 2015

Our heroine opens her eyes to the sound of her daughter in her still-sleepy face: "Mom, don't forget to pack my boots and call the school to tell them I am a parent pick-up today instead of a bus rider. And also, have you seen my library book? I can't find it. Miss Laurie said we were going to have to pay for it if we don't return it this week."

Our heroine thinks this is too much information to be exchanged before she has coffee, so she pulls herself up and into a sweatshirt and slippers before shuffling into the kitchen to get some. There she finds her oldest son already awake and sitting at the table playing a video game and also her husband, who has blessedly gotten up before her because he knows she is not good in the mornings. Also, he has already had his coffee.

She then goes downstairs to wake her youngest son who, upon opening his eyes, screams that he can't possibly get up because he has "not been snuggled yet!" She laughs and gets into bed with him, grateful for the request but also stifling a small aneurysm because she knows the bus is on the way. After some cajoling, she helps him pick out some clothes only to discover that all six pairs of pants hanging in his closet have holes in the knees, whereupon her six-year-old son declares he is sorry, but that "it's the gym class's fault." She picks a pair of jeans she hopes will pass for "purposely distressed."

Upstairs, she lays out vitamins and medications and pulls lunch bags from the fridge to be packed. After directing a line of questions that include: (1) "Have you brushed your teeth?" (2) "Have you made your bed?" and (3) "Have you packed your bag?" she looks at the clock, and realizes she has exactly three minutes to make it to the bus stop. Half-eaten waffles are shoved into little hands, and three children are packed into the car. As the bus arrives, the children ask her to wait to pull away from the stop sign so they can wave to her once they are on the bus. It is 7:55 a.m.

Back in the house, our heroine goes downstairs to find all the lights on in the children's bedrooms and not a single bed made, despite having told them to turn off their lights and make their beds. She empties both hampers to start a load of laundry, fills the dogs' bowls with food, and returns to the kitchen to do the breakfast dishes. There she discovers that her oldest son has forgotten his saxophone. Again. She opens her calendar to review the week and sees he has lacrosse practice, all three have youth group at church, and her daughter has a riding lesson. Her husband also tells her he will be leaving tomorrow and will be gone until Friday. Once she runs the vacuum in the front hall and makes her own bed, she sits down to write. There, she discovers that the printer is out of ink because her daughter has been printing coloring pages from her computer. Again.

At lunchtime, she is still in her pajamas and eating a yogurt at her desk while she pays bills online and submits an article on parenting. Somehow, the organization to which she is submitting the article thinks she is qualified to write it. But she considers that "qualified" and "survived" sound close enough to be confused and maybe that's how she got the assignment.

The phone rings at 12:42 p.m., and her daughter tells her from the office phone at school that she has a headache and a tummy ache. The nurse then gets on the phone to explain to our heroine that while her daughter has neither vomited nor is running a fever, would she be so kind as to come and pick her up from school?

Begrudgingly, our heroine puts on the same shirt and jeans that she wore yesterday and drives to school to retrieve her daughter, who it seems is not actually sick but in need of some time with Mom, so she spends the afternoon snuggling with her and watching a movie. This will require at least thirty minutes of self-talk on her part to quash the rising panic that she had a plan for today and her daughter's *admittedly fake* illness is screwing it all up. Two hours later, she picks the boys up from the bus stop, and when they get home she tells them to bring in their bags, paperwork, and jackets from the car. They do none of this. Eventually, each child is spread out in the kitchen while our heroine makes snacks, reviews tests and quizzes, and assists with homework. She heats chicken nuggets, tater tots, and frozen peas for dinner and at 6:00 p.m. shoves her husband and oldest son out the door to her son's lacrosse practice. While they are gone, our heroine makes lunches and sets the coffeemaker for the next day while breaking up a fight between her youngest two children and feeding the dogs their dinner.

At 8:00 p.m. everyone is marched through the shower in military fashion, bedtime snacks are had, and all three children are tucked into bed. She is harkened back four times before the bedrooms go quiet. She and her husband collapse into bed at 9:45 and watch an hour of TV before they both nod off. At 2:32 a.m. she gets up to use the bathroom and trips over a remote control car her youngest has left in her room. She also learns too late that one of the home's male residents has forgotten to put the toilet seat up while going potty. Again. In fact, it appears this male has not only forgotten to put the seat up but has also forgotten to turn on a light, or for that matter even point himself in the general direction of the toilet. So she feels her way in the dark to the dresser where she pulls out a dry pair of socks to switch out for the ones she's wearing. Because they are wet. Again.

• • • • •

I turned thirty and suddenly everyone was kind of hinting that I had to make something with my body. My husband was not questioned like this. As though I could snap my fingers and plant a baby that minute, I was run ragged with questions about when the "babies" were coming. My family and I live in Maryland, about an hour north of Baltimore city. But I look Midwestern. And there is a definite Midwestern "look," something between big-boned and the appearance of just having milked something. A roundness of face, a paleness of skin, and an ability to ask questions in a way that drives my mother-in-law crazy because they are grammatically incorrect but totally appropriate in Wisconsin. Questions like, "Are you going with us tomorrow, or no?" I also still call your East Coast water fountains "bubblers." I am fond of fried fish on a Friday night. But that's largely where the similarity to my Wisconsin friends ends. Most of them settled, married, and procreated early. I came in blazing to our ten-year reunion like I was headed to a rave. Most of them were content to sit and talk like grown-ups, because that's what grown-ups do.

Now, with three kids in tow and fifteen years of marriage behind us, our family is just your average bunch of weirdos next door. We're not running a fight club in our basement or anything, but we're different. Every family is. That's part of the wonder of all this. On television, it looks like we're all the same, with a couple of kids, a Labrador retriever, and a minivan. But behind closed doors there are a million variations. I am possibly quite weirder than you, even. Our family's atmospherics practically scream it.

Yesterday, Noah played his saxophone to accompany Grace as she attempted handstands off an exercise ball. One honk for each handstand. For an *hour*. I found six-year-old Jesse facedown in my pillow the other day, knees and hands tucked underneath him so that he made a little ball.

Q: "What are you doing, Jesse?"

A: "Smelling your love, Mama!"

He went on to work on a craft project later in the day, musing to himself as he worked, "This is hard but exciting. I feel so alive!"

On the first snow day of the past school year, my three children, lacking for any activity other than their mother telling them she would put on a movie or turn on the Playstation, decided to make their own fun. As I was washing the breakfast dishes, I heard all three of them singing Matthew Wilder's '80s classic "Break My Stride (Got to Keep

85

on Movin')" in unison as they carried Grace's Barbie dream house up from the playroom. I asked my oldest where they had heard the song and was simply told, "In our heads."

See what I mean? Awesome. And beautifully weird.

Part of our family's uniqueness is due to the fact that both boys are high-functioning autistics. This contributes to their behavior, as does the OCD, ADHD, and ODD (oppositional defiance disorder) that go along with their autism. It will cost us an average of $17,000 more a year, per boy, to raise them (thanks for the neat stats, Centers for Disease Control). We get a lot of ups and downs as far as how they interact with us and with each other. But they love to be on stage. Both boys think they are expert at everything. My daughter makes it her life's mission to prove they are not.

My husband works from home but travels constantly, so I'm never certain when, exactly, I will see him. When I do see him, our work schedules sometimes overlap. Sometimes they just downright collide. I have the great privilege of being a writer and spending whatever time I want in my pajamas. But after a while, I actually do like to get dressed. Matt does not care about trivialities like clothes. For him there exists no distinction between workout clothes, sleep clothes, and day clothes. And working side by side with him can be alternatingly sweet and repulsive. When he paces into my office on his cell phone during a work call (as he loves to pace when he is talking), I debate chucking a shoe at him. I need total silence when I'm writing, because it takes a truckload of brain power for me to come up with something that makes sense. Matt, though, can talk to someone on his phone, someone on Skype, and someone sitting next to him, all at the same time. Though not well, I would add.

I'm kind of a mother-worker hybrid, which also makes me a bit unconventional. Because I spend a lot of time in a part of my house, in front of a computer that's always around, and because when my kids are sick or home from school I am the one to take care of them while also trying to write in that part of the house, I am just out of the realm of most working mothers. I'm kind of always "around." My children have a hard time understanding that I am trying to accomplish something when I sit down at my desk. I wonder if putting on an actual pair of pants would change things.

We aren't truly suburbanites either. We live in the middle of the country and we have no family around. Going anywhere or doing anything requires quite a scramble to cover childcare. Then there's the fact that my husband is kind of a bon vivant. If he could throw a party every day, he would. He is a Southerner with a penchant for country music, pro wrestling, and barbecue. Though I've lived in Maryland some fifteen-odd years, I own a foam cheese head, couldn't tell you the lyrics to a single country song, and still say "restaurant" like there's an "o" in it. I love riding horses and will sing opera on a dare, though my favorite music is the songs my kids beg me to sing for them before bed. I tolerate a lot of barbecue and also a dirty house because I can't get anyone to buy into the concept that it's nice to know where things actually are. Our house is loud, our front door is always open, and everybody hollers. Everybody but me. I love my noise-canceling headphones.

Our family also keeps counselors and pharmacists in business. This is so my husband and I don't poison each other's iced tea with arsenic. It is also so that my son doesn't send himself into a panic attack at school. Even our dogs are uncommon. No garden-variety Labradors or Golden Retrievers. We have three (because we saw no problem with outnumbering the adults by both kids *and* pets): a Shiba Inu, a Texas Heeler, and a Borzoi. The only breed we didn't consider was a Cane Corso, the one that looks like a big, wrinkly horse. The one that was once bred to kill people. Bred for murder equals deal breaker.

Really, nothing we do is simple. Or common. We're kind of high-living survivalists. Imagine Robert Peary on the first expedition to the North Pole if he showed up with an entourage and a grill. The frostbite's going to kill them, but they're going to party like it won't.

•   •   •   •   •

As a mother, as a member of the people-making tribe, I sometimes segregate myself in certain unintentional ways. I believe all mothers do. This is due to the uniqueness of every child and the uniqueness of every woman. We, all of us, will parent in very different ways. Some of us hover while others lock our children outside when the weather is nice and yell at them through the window to "Go burn off some energy." Some of us swear by gluten-free organic foods while others spend money in the produce aisle and then have to toss the spinach in the garbage because it wasn't eaten before it liquefied. Some of us work while others stay home with our children. Some, like me, do both. All of us are potentially the weirdos next door.

But children are so utterly delicious. And this infatuated, bottomless, senseless love is what connects us as mothers.

I haven't for one moment looked at my three sprouts and not thought about gobbling them up. Two of them have dimples, two of them have freckles, and all of them have blonde hair and blue eyes. They laugh like fairies even when they are choking and punching each other like tweaked-out trolls. But they are so wonderfully, imperfectly perfect, and I love them so dearly that I want to nibble their sweet skin and smooth cheeks and stubby toes until they are eaten right up. I cannot get enough of their hugs and kisses. My family and I have taken to calling this phenomenon a "cute attack." It's that thing when you love something so much that you just want to squeeze it to death. When Max tells the wild things he's beating feet in Maurice Sendak's *Where the Wild Things Are*, they cry big monstrous tears and tell him they'll eat him up, they love him so. This is a legitimate psychological response, by the by.[1] I promise you I am not a serial killer.

I start with this premise because this infatuation with my children, this manifestation of the I-love-you-so-much-I-can-barely-stand-it kind of love is how I imagine all mothers feel. Why else do all mothers at some point try to shove our baby's hand or pudgy foot into our mouths? We love with such intensity it's almost too much to take. I get excited every time I see the school bus barreling toward our house (and it does barrel; I'm not sure they give speeding tickets to bus drivers, but sister needs to slow down). I cannot wait to hug and kiss and squeeze them. Until the screaming starts about ten minutes after they're home, and at that point I want to run out of the house to go find that bus so I can throw them back on.

We adore our children. And they adore us too. This passionate commitment to people other than ourselves, this selfless bond connects us to our children. And it connects us to each other as women. We are part of a sisterhood of having brought people into the world and loving them with all we have.

I remember reading *The Yearling* by Marjorie Kinnan Rawlings decades ago. I only recall the basics of the story, except for one passage I can recite from memory: Jody has argued with his mother, and when they reconcile, Rawlings describes how Jody tenderly touches his mother's "downy cheek." I found the use of the word *downy* strange when I first read it. Was Jody's mother a rabbit? Of course, now that I am in my forties and I have down *on my own cheeks*, I realize it was the perfect adjective. Unfortunately.

I don't know why this paragraph stuck with me so firmly through the years, but I recalled it immediately when my then ten-year-old Noah lay curled in the half moon of my body on the bed.

Ten minutes earlier, he'd blown up at me. Matt had been traveling again, and I sent him a message.

HELP ME. Kids WILL NOT go to bed.

It was 9:20 on a school night. The kids were nowhere near bed. (The time is approximate. The number of capital letters is exact.)

Matt called two minutes later.

"Put me on speaker. I will talk to them."

In an apparent crossing of wires, Noah blew up because, he explained, he was going to bed. It just wasn't as fast as I had wanted him to. So when I bent over to kiss him goodnight, he put his hand up to block the kiss I tried to lay on his neck. I wasn't going to fight it. Five minutes later, he popped out of the shadows upstairs as I was trying to close the house up.

He stammered, "Can I talk to you in private?" There was, of course, no one around. Unless he was referring to my ghost—the one he'd scared right out of my body by pulling his sudden appearing act in the dark.

He teared up and said, "Can you say good night to me again? I want to do it over."

I brought him to bed to cuddle, and in our quiet moment Noah said, "I will tell you something about my day!" as he absentmindedly reached up to pet my cheek. Yes, even the downy part. But when he did it I remembered the passage from *The Yearling* and also when I had petted my own grandmother's cheek as I would lay with her on the bed in her condo in Illinois, telling her about my own day. I may need to get that fuzz sandblasted off someday, but when my not-too-old-to-cuddle son petted it quietly, I smiled with newfound appreciation for my weird body. I smiled also because of the love I had for my son, connected by years and shared experience to all mothers everywhere.

I know other mothers have found themselves digging in during this path, trying to shuffle through the parenting rubble enough to find out what it is that they are doing underneath it all. Yes, you are raising humans. This is understood. You are prompting them, protecting them, promoting them toward independence and functionality. But is it enough? Because it seems so very, very far ahead of us on the journey. Even for those of us who are past it, those whose children are out and gone away, doing what they were designed to do, it can be startling to look back on one's life and think, *Did all this have value?*

God permits us to step into this job, the one with breathtaking changes and strange additions. We need not interview or apply. He simply chooses us and we step into it as he has planned. But so much of it is attended by wondering, and quiet questions surface when God begins to form our children within us. God, who also made us within our own mothers' wombs (see Job 31:15). A miracle, on repeat. One that comes with questions, as all miracles do.

What is the worth of doing motherhood? Of being their person, their singular greatest influence for so many long, hard years? How do you calculate the value of being the picker-upper, the driver, the cleaner, the cooker, and the nose-wiper?

Especially when the old things are falling away and you've entered this long, weird stretch of undefined wasteland?

• • • • •

My body was the first thing to get weird. While I was aware this would happen, I didn't realize the extent to which weirdness was possible. *What to Expect When You're Expecting* may as well be titled *Kiss Your Body Good-Bye*. There will be a part of you (and if you're lucky, many parts of you) that will be permanently altered after children. Of course, by "lucky," I mean "cursed."

I developed *melasma*, also known delightfully as the "mask of pregnancy." Like I was Jason from *Friday the 13th*. Nobody wants the word *mask* in their pregnancy lexicon. Then there was the *linea negra*, another delightful color code that some knocked-up women bear—that line from belly button to underside. Very helpful in case my doctor decided she'd lost her way on the path to the baby's exit route. My feet swelled so that I wore flip-flops everywhere, not that I cared because I was no longer aware of what my feet looked like after a certain point. After baby? It was a memorable number of stitches, and a belly I could practically fold in half. Oh, and bleeding nipples. Whoever tells you nursing is easy is under the influence of drugs. They are probably drugs she's getting because she is in so much pain from nursing. Also, the bigger your baby, the hungrier it will be and the more it will want to nurse. So do the math. My stomach skin is still like crepe paper, and while in clothes it doesn't look half bad, I would need the promise of a college fund for my kids just to bend over in a bikini in front of anyone but my husband.

Another thing that got weird was my attitude toward other people. I am conciliatory to a near fault, but something about the wash of postpartum hormones had me livid when, for example, people who promised to babysit or deliver a meal to help us with our new life adjustment didn't make good on their word. I realize now how ridiculous this was, because I'm fairly convinced there are people still waiting for meals from me based on promises I delivered in 2012. (I once delivered a "baby" gift for a friend's child who had already started walking by the time it got to him.)

When you're not living in immediate proximity to someone else, life has an annoying tendency to get in the way. I believe the Lord gave me lots of practice in being patient with other people because I would someday need other people to exhibit lots of patience with me. One of survival's gifts is that it teaches you the extent of your own stamina. Like your stamina to eat cereal for dinner every night for a week because no one's signed up to deliver a meal and you can't bear the thought of putting a frozen pizza in the oven because all the dial turning, box opening, and waiting is just too much to take.

And God help Matt. He was (mostly) unfairly the target of my enigmatic, hormone-induced rage. As I woke up in the middle of the night for the one-bazillionth nursing session, I would silently glare at the sleeping form of my husband next to me. Matt did, in fact, rise in the middle of the night with Noah to change him and hand him to me before going back to sleep. But by the time Grace and Jesse rolled around, I'm sure he was pretty much like, *Eh, the crib's on her side of the bed anyway.*

By the way, Matt, I love you and you're an awesome dad.

There was also the unexpected obsession about Noah's safety and doing baby things "right" after I had him. I sanitized and purged and bleached like I was working in an Ebola ward. No one could touch him without disinfected hands. If a pacifier fell on the ground, it had to be thrown away. If the wipes warmer didn't warm the wipes sufficiently, its sponge had to be special-ordered from a specific website. No activities were permitted during baby's nap time, and all schedules were set accordingly. I trusted no one to watch him until he was six months old and beyond the age of SIDS risk.

Then, as is the case with subsequent children, it was pretty much filthy hands, cold wipes, cat naps in the car, and babysitters as soon as I could pump enough milk to skedaddle for a few hours. And guess what? All three of them survived. I have more baby mementoes for Noah, but I was a lot more relaxed—and quite possibly a happier mom—with Noah's younger siblings.

My body became weird; our family is weird; and my preferences, likes, and dislikes are weird. Yours are, too, I'll bet. But I look back now and realize that the oddities of motherhood are part of the wilds. Everything is strange when it's unexpected, and so much of motherhood is just plain being caught by surprise. I've probably passed you, out here, somewhere on the way to your scrapbooking group.

Good on you. I'm going to turn the TV on for my kids and take a nap.

nine

Play Nice

Part of what's surprised me about motherhood has very little to do with kids at all. I've discovered (or maybe simply seen with new eyes) how mean women can be to one another. Men do it too, certainly. But there's a different strategy employed by women in conflict. I find that for the most part, men just confront each other outright. There's lots of shoulder shrugging, and sometimes the bro-hug when things are patched up. It's all very straightforward.

I've yet to find a man who can fight like a woman. Have you ever seen a hero in a movie "talk out" his fight with his estranged mother or his best friend? That's because a man in the cinema will pull a gun, whereas a woman is content to stir a pot of lit matches and then dump a bunch of kerosene in it. Sometimes we do it right. When we're focusing on others and not ourselves, we remember to follow Matthew 5:22, 24, which says, "Everyone who is angry with his brother will be liable to judgment. . . . First be reconciled to your brother" (ESV).

But then there is the snarky-texting, double entendre–wielding, Facebook-posting, cutting-each-other-out-of-the-group kind of mean. I'm talking the kind of silent antipathy that makes us different fighters than men, the part that holds on to a grudge like Gollum holds the Ring and says one thing to your face but something completely different behind your back. This is the gossipy, snide kind of mean. This is the part that when asked, "What's wrong?" answers, "Oh, nothing," and then un-friends you on Facebook, which you discover by accident when you go to "like" one of her pictures. Women can change something as simple as their tone of voice or their use of language to communicate more than a man usually can with a podium and a megaphone. Women can be kind of scary, and they can be mean.

Unfortunately, this meanness really has an opportunity to blossom in motherhood. Nowhere will a woman's insecurities take center stage the way they do in parenting. And insecurities can make for one mean mother.

My theory? When a woman has a child, the infinite possibilities of her life are narrowed somewhat. One day, she may have nothing in common with her friend. They may like different music or different foods and be different ages or from different backgrounds. Their tastes may differ on hundreds of levels, and their professions may span all possibilities. But when a woman has a child, one critically important part of her life—her distinction as a mother—is now shared with literally millions of other women. And women always have opinions. Millions of opinions. These opinions usually involve a belief that the way we do things is the best way.

Enter mommy-shaming. Starting from conception and moving forward in one mercenary wave, the shaming begins with the choice of childbearing method. Natural or epidural? Midwife or hospital? Water birth? Home birth?

I didn't trust myself to create an environment in my home that was going to bring another person safely into the world without contracting smallpox. I know people did this all the time a hundred years ago, but a lot more people also died in childbirth a hundred years ago. As it turned out, a hospital was the best possible choice for us. I like clean, white, disinfected hospitals, and I like doctors who've studied the process of human beings being born for a very long time before they get around to me. I like the fact that I know my doctor has plenty of initials after her name, because as far as I'm concerned, it minimizes the odds of a birth experience becoming the Hindenburg disaster, with something going down and not well.

Noah was a week late, and I had a partial placenta previa for the last few weeks of my pregnancy. This was a condition that, thankfully, righted itself before my water broke in the middle of the dead heat of a cicada-choked summer. This summer, the bugs were so loud that my moaning on the way to the car was barely audible. I'm sure my neighbors were grateful for this. I was only two centimeters dilated and told to walk around the hospital to get things going. So I walked, and walked. And I only got to three centimeters after about two hours of pacing, but I was ready to punch the nurse in the face when she begrudgingly admitted me, telling me that I was making "too much noise" for the state of labor I was in.

"You're only three centimeters," she said with a sneer. "You shouldn't be hurting that much yet."

I was now in my eighth hour of contractions, and snapped back, "I don't know how I'm supposed to feel, because this is my first baby, but I can tell you that *this hurts*!"

I was admitted, and according to my ridiculous type A birth plan I was planning on refusing pain medication. Yes, listen ye medical professionals to this roaring lioness of a woman as she brings life into the world.

As it turns out, they did hear me roar, as did the patients on the opposite wing, because guess what? There was so much scar tissue on that cervix of mine that my doctor said, "Well, no wonder you're not dilating! Everything is stuck!" I wanted her to call up that nurse and tell her to go suck an egg because she hadn't assessed my pain level correctly the first time. Ha! Apparently I *could* hurt "that much!"

Then my doctor said something I have not yet forgotten.

"So, we have two options. We can wait for it to snap open on its own by giving you Pitocin to increase the contraction rate." (Oh, dear Lord, the pain was going to come *faster*?) "Or I can go in and break the scar tissue for you."

What's that now? You want to break something?

Break is not a word that a woman in the throes of labor wants to hear. I don't want to hear about breaking anything, unless it's a bottle of champagne against the hull of a ship they name in my honor because I was obviously going to be a hero after this nightmare of a birthing experience.

"PITOCIN!" I screamed at her. "Pitocin, Pitocin, Pitocin!"

So here came the meds to up the ante, and I also tried Demerol to take the edge off. I didn't want the epidural. I was convinced things weren't going to take much longer, so I decided to wait it out. The whole circus had started at 7:30 a.m. on Thursday. It was now 1:00 a.m. Friday.

After another hour, I was screaming for an epidural. So much for the birth plan.

Noah was delivered at 1:35 p.m. on Friday afternoon. If you're counting, that's thirty hours of labor, including four and a half hours of pushing. He became stuck in the birth canal, his heart rate dropped, an internal fetal scalp monitor was applied, there was talk of an emergency C-section, somebody grabbed a forceps, and finally, there was a conversation with my husband about how I just really wanted to go to sleep and couldn't somebody just pull him out and wake me up when it was over? Why was this whole thing so hard?

Because that fat turkey of a baby weighed nine pounds when he was born, and evidently birthing a small Clydesdale isn't as easy as it looks in the movies.

When we had Jesse, our youngest, things went—as they often do after the highway has been paved by previous children—blisteringly fast. We were approached during the brief early hours of labor by the chief of obstetric nursing, who asked if we might be amenable to one of the young male nursing students observing the birth.

Let me tell you, once you've had your undercarriage examined by everybody but the janitor while enough people for a baseball team mill around the room, one more person doesn't faze you a bit. We agreed. Mike, the aforementioned nursing student, stood sheepishly at the entrance to the room while the delivery was taking place, and at one point turned so white and wavered so noticeably on his feet that Matt called out to ask him if he was ok. Which kind of peeved me, because while I don't think I'm a narcissist, it seems that if there is going to be one opportunity to focus *solely* on your wife, it's when she's pushing your son out of her body. But whatever.

Jesse was delivered in twenty minutes flat, and when they laid him on my chest, I cooed and cried and kissed his slick face. Two hours later, as I wrapped the tiny package of his body in my arms and prayed over him and his new life, Mike came back into the room.

"I just wanted to thank you," he said.

"For what?" I asked.

"For letting me . . . you know, um, come in and be there. I mean . . . it was just the most amazing . . ." He held his hands out, stumbling for an accurate description.

"Miraculous?" I smiled at him.

He paused.

"Yes . . . that's it—miraculous."

Disagreements about methods of birthing are utterly useless. The most important takeaway is that the whole thing is miraculous. I praise God for the knowledge and work of my hospital, because Noah's complicated birth may not have resulted in a happy ending if we'd tried it at home or with a midwife. This isn't to say mine is the "better" way. If you've brought a human into the world, you have been privy to one of God's great mysteries. The Lord could have chosen any way to perpetuate our species. But he picked women and our bodies. What a blessing and a gift. You have been the vessel for a great and beautiful enigma. Yours is a story of great worth. You are the ultimate chaperone, the bringer of life into the world. Be proud of that, no matter the method you will choose or have chosen.

* * * * *

If you do have strong feelings about preferred birthing methods, it's nearly guaranteed you'll also have them about the bottle vs. breastfeeding debate.

I was committed to breastfeeding. Cheap, easy, portable, healthy—what's not to love? Except that no one told me that every time I nursed for the first few weeks it was going to feel like someone slashed me with razor blades and poured lemon juice on the cuts. And when your baby is nine pounds, he is hungry a lot, so you have to nurse a lot, even when you're scabbed and/or bleeding. The lactation Nazis in the hospital were coming into the room every hour to check on how things were going and were getting all handsy in the process, which I intensely disliked because the epidural had worn off and along with it my complete abandon about body boundaries.

I was starting to hurt, the sheets were back up over my knees, the lights were low, my body was back to being sort of my own again—and I was not thrilled by a stranger reaching into my hospital gown to make sure I was doing things the "right way." It took quite awhile to get things working in the right order and at the right time. Then of course there were the ovals of shame when I frequently leaked through my bra and into my shirt. Also? All my children loved to peek out from behind the "hooter hider" that I thought was the greatest invention known to man. Until it was utterly useless. My children would be in full lunch mode, and I would naturally be in public, and then a little hand would pull back the flimsy cloth curtain to expose more of me to the world than God or anyone intended.

I nursed Noah until he was a year old, because as you may have already suspected by now, nursing gets easier. God made our bodies as not only transporters for other people but also suppliers of their actual sustenance. Which is also kind of amazing. Some women have no difficulty whatsoever nursing. Others, like one of my friends, have a body construction you would think gave them their own dairy store and yet can't produce enough to feed an infant who was born two pounds lighter than mine. Sometimes it just doesn't work. And you know what? Formula is fine. I had to learn this and get over the guilt of not being able to nurse Jesse beyond five months when I became really sick with a rare disease and required all sorts of tests and chemicals and medications to nail down a diagnosis and a cure. They were injecting me with radioactive dye to test my innards, and I was strictly prohibited from nursing. The doctors were all like, "Don't nurse, or your baby is going to develop horns and a tail."

I realized there were moms who had to choose bottle feeding over breastfeeding because something in their lives prevented them from nursing. And Jesse made up for this loss of nursing time by being attached to my hip at every waking moment. He still is. At six years old. Matt can't get him dressed for school until he's had his "snuggle time" with me in the morning. I got back all that nursing closeness in spades.

On a likewise competitive, why-are-grown-women-being-so-mean-to-each-other note, you can take your Pinterest posts and shove them. I do not want to see your perfect, hand-stenciled birthday party invitations, or your fall party cupcakes in the shape of a three-dimensional ear of corn. This is why I am not on Pinterest. Because Pinterest is designed to make every woman feel like a failure unless that woman is Rachael Ray, whom I'm sure has a great Pinterest account that she feels great about, but I wouldn't know in either case because I'm not on Pinterest. I once posted a picture on Facebook of an apple pie I made. And then I thought, *Why did I just post a picture of a pie? So other women can be impressed?* Because there wasn't a guy I know who was going to look twice at a picture of a pie. Except for Matt, who ate half of the actual thing in one sitting. I think there should be a rule that if you post something stellar you've made on social media, you should also post directions on how to do it, and those directions should make it easy. As in, "You could do this in five minutes" easy. Or, "I actually just bought this from a store and heated it up" easy.

Another thing that makes mothers everywhere feel about as worthless as these domestic-goddess social media posts do are the body criticisms. Please do not brag to every woman you know about how you (1) have time for a regular mani-pedi, (2) dropped all the baby weight in three weeks without the help of a celebrity trainer, and/or (3) don't leave the house without makeup or unless you're totally put together. I gained an entire recliner-full of weight with Noah, and it took me eighteen months to lose it. And then I got pregnant again, so the whole getting-fat cycle repeated itself. Immediately. The last time I got a pedicure was a year ago. I'm not exaggerating, either. If anyone's feet need work, they're mine. My daughter has called them "aliens," my son has said they're "weird." There's probably a medical term for what's going on, but I'll never know because I don't have time to go to the podiatrist. I just shove my sweaty feet into closed-toe shoes even in summer, because they look like they were carved by a drunken stonemason.

As for appearances? I once held—early on, and before real life and real motherhood got the best of me—to the belief that Matt would come home to a showered, well-dressed lady of the manor with faultless makeup. This was naturally ridiculous. It was possible for a short time, because Noah's sole activities after his birth and for the first two months of his life were eating and sleeping. I had a lot of shower-ing and dressing time. Today? I have school-aged children but am still home as a unique variety of housewife-writer, and nearly left the house in my pajamas when I got the call this morning that my son was puking in the nurse's office. I changed only because tripping over my slippers on the way to the door woke me from my sleepy writer's reverie and I realized I had to get dressed. I did not for one second con-sider putting on makeup, even to cover a pimple (yes, you *can* still get pimples in your forties!), and the most prepared I got for human contact was to slip on a pair of jeans and brush my teeth.

Let us celebrate each other when we have been able to dress nicely or work out or reach a personal goal. Let us otherwise forget the bragging and the shaming and admit to ourselves that we've worn sweatpants to a parent-teacher conference or forgotten to wear deodorant more than once.

Dr. Wednesday Martin, an anthropologist with degrees from Yale and extensive experience in studying group dy-namics, moved to the upper east side of New York with her children after becoming a stay-at-home mom, or SAHM.[1] In this part of the concrete jungle, she discovered the rari-fied trophy wife: the educated woman who had given up her career to stay at home with her children. These women had established a kind of deified pursuit of childrearing in which their appearance was a direct statement of their capability. The most successful received an annual "wife bonus" for a job well done, to wit: raising the kids, managing the house, and looking good at society galas. Full blowouts, makeup, and high heels were worn to student drop-off, where there was a cavalcade of Cadillacs parked three deep. These women were self-organized by perceived rank, with Hermes Birken bags in hand, and took to engaging picky eater coaches for their kids; organizing elaborate, exclusive playdates; and enrolling their children in preschools with $24,000 yearly tuitions.

These women are obviously aliens. And with the convenient calculation of a "wife bonus" that feels like a salary, maybe they don't often struggle with the determination of their value.

Yet their insecurities in having made sacrifices that required pausing their own professional aspirations and relying on their husbands to make the household income were the vibrating theme in Martin's study. Even with a "bonus," the sacrifice of career for family stung a bit. Having become "nothing more" than SAHMs, these aliens introduce the mother of all mom-shaming trends.

This is the discussion that sparks a hotter fire than any dialogue on the necessity of organic food or the rightness of co-sleeping. It is the stay-at-home mom vs. working mom debate. Nothing gets moms lined up on the sidelines like an argument about whether SAHMs are better mothers than working moms because SAHMs are the only ones available to their children 24/7.

●　●　●　●　●

I will say this: I didn't have any intention of staying home with Noah. Being a traditionalist, I surprised everyone with this. I had found my sweet spot at the advertising agency with fabulous people, fun work, and a comfortable salary.

I had also become set on the idea of my worth being inextricably linked to what I did for a living. Still committed to setting random bars, I was able to tell people that I was "in-house counsel and business development manager," which sounded like I had value. I sounded important—not if I were up against a neurosurgeon, maybe, but it was sufficient everyday career currency. And so I went on to set another arbitrary guideline for myself when the time came to make a decision about what would happen at the conclusion of this nine-month sea-monkey project taking place in my uterus.

Revenue at the agency had become a struggle, and much like the other staff, I hadn't had a raise in two years. *How much can they value me*, I mused, *if they're not willing to do what it takes to keep me around?* I determined that if, before taking my maternity leave (coinciding with the end of the fiscal year), I received at least a cost of living wage increase, I would stay with the agency and find childcare for Noah.

This was preposterous. Why? Because I was making a decision without knowing how I would be blindsided by one of motherhood's great surprises: the sheer volume of burning, protective, all-consuming love I would have for my child after he was born.

We sold stock, traded in our car, and downsized every way we knew how so that I could wheel my newborn down the hall of the ad agency to my boss's office and tell him thank you for the opportunity, but I would be leaving to stay at home with my son.

His response came out as a jumble of, "Wait—are you kidding me? Wow. I mean, that's a real shock. I don't—just . . . wow." He clearly hadn't seen it coming. Neither of us had.

Parenthetically, I never did get a raise. But it wouldn't have mattered anyway.

After the initial, endorphin-driven high of newborn motherhood began to wane and I found no difference between what I wore when sleeping and what I wore when awake, I entered the empty days of feeling like I was doing nothing but keeping myself and Noah alive and had dark moments of wondering whether I'd done the right thing. Whether I could actually be a stay-at-home mother after all.

Too late, sister.

But things, as they do because they're ordered by a God whose way is perfect (see Ps. 18:30), worked out exactly as they should have. Six months after I turned in my resignation, the agency was acquired by another, bigger firm that laid off approximately 60 percent of the staff, including many of my co-workers in the corporate portion of the business. I not only made the best decision for our family, I received total confirmation from the Lord that it was the right choice. It was as if I had been given the chance to look back at the train station as I was safely down the tracks and watch the whole platform explode into flames.

However, I know that not all women are as fortunate as I am. Some women have to work. For some families, finances create a barrier to giving up the workplace for the home place. Childcare is expensive, unless you're going to hire a stranger off Craigslist for five dollars an hour and make them bring their own food. Once you factor in extras like transportation, wardrobe, and car maintenance for all those hours you're logging by going in to the office, the decision to stay home becomes the obvious one for lots of women. In other situations, childcare may be more accessible and affordable, and the salary of a working mom might greatly outweigh the cost savings of staying at home.

A working mom may get a coffee break and a chance to take her time in the bathroom, but a SAHM doesn't necessarily have to take a shower or get dressed every day. I have gone long days in the same outfit. I have tested the limits of both my own tolerance and the strength of my family's olfactory nerves. Both are impressively high.

A working mom gets the praise from her boss for a job well done, or the satisfaction of a completed task that she can look at and admire. A SAHM is there at the exact moment a first step is taken. If I were working, I might get to have a nice lunch with my co-workers, but now I can lie in bed and watch SpongeBob with my six-year-old when he's sick and not have to call a babysitter in a panic.

There are uncomfortable sacrifices that both SAHMs and working moms have to endure. There are hard parts and easy parts for each of us. There are the benefits and breathers we get, and the migraines and monsters that also come. But ultimately, both choices are made to benefit our children. One relates to time and one relates to finances. And to her great credit, the working mom doesn't get to come home and turn it off, either. It's not like her kids are going to get her the paper, her slippers, and the TV remote so she can kick back after a stressful day. Someone still has to help with homework and make sure they don't starve to death.

While conflicting studies propose that either quantity of time or quality of time is preferred in parenting, ultimately motherhood's nucleus is time.[2] Whether it's a lot of time or focused time, children require that their parents be present. I have been blessed to be able to give my children the gift of my undiluted presence. Though I'll be the first to admit, the time they get isn't always of the highest quality. Sometimes, it has been the quality of a half-awake ogre with the breath to match. Grace can attest to this. She has no difficulty whatsoever letting me know when I am less than fresh and grossing her out. Too bad. That's what she gets for waking me before dawn.

If I had gone back to work, I might have missed out on some of the daily magic that seeps into the everyday doing of motherhood, magic that springs forth *ex nihilo*. The magic is some of what God gives to mothers, and I believe it is his "thank you." I feel as though these tiny idylls are part of what sustain us when things are hard and bleak.

During one particular night, Jesse came stumbling into our bedroom. He was sobbing that heart-wrenching sob that to this day rends my heart. He cried that his stomach was hurting, but not before he could walk all the way around to my side of the bed and puke all over my sheets. And his mother. A mom who has endured a nighttime bout with the stomach flu will understand what kind of cleanup and resettling was required. Too fried to take him back downstairs, I put a sleepy Jesse back to bed between Matt and me and prayed for a puke truce.

The next morning, Jesse put his face directly in mine and stage-whispered, "You and Dad were snoring like hogs last night!"

"Shhhhmmmmmhmhm," I groaned. "Mommy's still asleep."

Then Jesse picked up my hand and started to pet it. I have always loved when my children play with me, and this, too, is a gift that sneaks up on you, despite and even because of the once-hideous sensation that your body is no longer your own. This is another wrapped blessing from God: when my daughter takes a brush to my hair and strokes down in long, smooth movements, or Noah tentatively reaches over to hold my hand while we are praying. Or when Jesse has crawled into my bed in the night and occupies himself for a few minutes while I try to wrestle my unwilling body out of sleep by performing a puppet show with my flaccid hands.

He wrestled them with his own, with his hand the victor, then mine. Then he turned toward my face again and said, "You know, I am sad because Uncle Sammy died, and I only got to see him once. He went at the wrong time, Mommy. I hope God takes care of him in heaven."

My eyes flew open. I was now very much awake. "Oh honey," I said, "of course he will! Uncle Sammy knew Jesus and we will see him again."

I realized at that moment that because I was lying in bed at 7:36 a.m. with my five-year-old son and not on my way to an office somewhere, I was offered a glimpse into heaven.

This arrangement of being home with my children has suited our family perfectly. Our choices work, and we believe God has blessed them greatly. Not knowing ahead of time what we'd have to experience, it was a good thing that I was home with our kids, because I could keep an eye on things that were troubling. Like the stunted rate of the boys' development or the fact that I regularly found Grace "experimenting" in my bathroom with the stuff women keep out of sight for a reason. My kids need a good amount of continual oversight. I'm convinced leaving them with a nanny would leave *me* with the charred shell of what used to be a house.

•   •   •   •   •

This mom-shaming business is totally ridiculous, because at some point, all of us wonder if we're doing a good job. This wondering actually proves we're great moms. Not-great moms don't worry about things like whether they are succeeding with their kids. You and I pack lunches, fold laundry, help with homework, and say bedtime prayers, and all of it is proof that we've answered a call from the Giver of these children to steward them carefully and well. Losing your temper or not being a room mom doesn't mean you've blown it. Neither does bottle feeding, birthing with a midwife at home, feeding them fast-food, or forgetting all the year-end school projects.

Year-end project, you say? My experience in failing them all is legend. So much so, in fact, that last week, as Grace and I were bent over a poster that she was supposed to do on Theodore Roosevelt *before* the actual day it was due, I didn't double-check her facts. And so it was that Grace went to school and proudly displayed her poster to her teacher bearing our twenty-sixth president's birthplace as Indiana and not New York. I would have caught this, I'm sure, if I hadn't been yelling out instructions to the boys in the other room as I also tried in vain to keep spray glue from sticking to Grace's hair. Also, I would like to know when kindergarteners got so much homework. Every week this year, Jesse came home with a packet the thickness of a refrigerator manual. At the end of May, I mutinied and just outright refused to open it. He gets a story every night. We count bugs and identify patterns. I make him write his name in birthday cards. Isn't that good enough?

Being a mother is hard not only because of the level of input but also because of the lack of direction we get in how to do it. You strain at some approach and hope the way you're doing things will pay off, even though your kids go to public school, or you let them watch too much TV, or they eat food with red dye no. 4. Whatever works for other moms, whatever authors tell you to do—those things may not work for your children. Because the tricky thing about kids is they're all different and they all have their own ideas. Now add to that how high the stakes are when we realize we are raising people who will have to go and be adults. They will vote and drive cars, they might have children of their own, and dear Lord, what if you're failing not only your own kids but generations after them? Can you think of a job with more pressure? (Maybe NASA engineer. Because, explosions.)

With the stakes so high, there are things all mothers do behind closed doors that contradict the wisdom we've been given by more mature parents. Bribes, negotiation, and in-consistency, for example. We know they're all bad for the child's construct. But I will tell you that, in secret, I use them all. Every. Last. One.

I didn't set out to parent this way. Things sort of fall to the universal law of fatigue when your brood keeps grow-ing. I honestly look at that Gosselin woman and wonder how in the name of sweet baby condors she's able to keep them all straight, with the whole army of them toeing the line. She might be a fabulous parent. But this also might be owing to the fact that there are cameras rolling. I can tell you, I would step up my game if I thought all my parenting moments were going to be broadcast on TLC. I would sure as sausage yell less.

Motherhood is also crazy-making. I can recite a list of things and people I couldn't stand after becoming a mother.

For example: the mention of scrapbooking made me want to throw myself off a bridge. Too much hyperbole? Okay. It made me want to throw a scrapbook off a bridge. It's an innocuous pursuit. Sweet, even. But here's what happened in my life with my trio. Noah, as the first child, got everything good. He has a baby book recalling his first steps and his first words, with pictures of him at every month. There is hair from his first haircut, tied with a tiny blue satin bow and slipped into a cellophane envelope. It's all terribly precious.

Then I had another baby, plus one more. And the whole scheme fell apart.

Do you know what Grace's first word was? How about Jesse's? I have no earthly idea, so if you remember, please tell me. I never wrote it down, and I have the memory of a coma patient who's just woken up. I am just one step removed from not remembering who the people are around me.

Scrapbooking was part of the motherhood experience that reminded me of my disappointing lack of time and ability at every corner, in addition to my frustration with not having been better at recording such a fleeting period of time in the young lives of my children. So I grew to hate it. But not anymore. Now, I admire the beautiful collections of my friends who get together in groups and build the most loving testimonies of their children in books that are as beautiful as they are sweet. I have built another testimony. I write different kinds of books. I figure it's a sufficient replacement for my nonexistent scrapbooking. The Lord reminds me that I am doing my best, and the scrapbooking mother is too. I love her and her beautiful creations. She and I bear the same badge of honor.

Another thing I disliked after motherhood's first step were the "joiners." Hear me out—my insecurities require me to counter the seeming awfulness of this statement. I am a member of the PTA but I rarely volunteer. I pay my dues so I can read the emails and notices about what is going on at my children's school. But that's it. And I *work from home* so it's not like I have to ask my boss for time off to do it.

The parents of the 1970s and 1980s did not attend every track practice. My folks dropped me off at track practice and picked me up when it was over. Do you know why? Because their identity wasn't wrapped up in their children. They did not feel compelled to dog us through every stage of life. They were content to let us do things by ourselves because that's the point of raising kids, anyway. You want your children to ultimately function on their own. Also, watching track practice is deathly boring. So is watching soccer practice, football practice, or lacrosse practice.

Matt and I differ here. He will attend every practice for every sport, and sometimes will even coach. He exerts actual effort and doesn't just sit on the sidelines and surf the internet (not all the time, anyway). I, however, will stay at home with whichever kids don't have practice and ready the house for the next morning—laundry, dishes, lunches. I will then sit my backside down on the couch and watch the national news. Because I am a grown-up, and the days of raising kids are long, and my son is going to be just fine if no one stands on the sideline of every practice.

I did musical theater as a fifth grader. My mother would bring a Tupperware container of dinner for me to eat at my break during rehearsals for *The Sound of Music* and then walk right back out the door. Because there were other kids and other things to do, and I was going to be just dandy on my own. But she was there on opening night with my father and my siblings. Which made her presence all the more special.

In this vein, I want to know when grade-schoolers were suddenly thrown into multiple activities. I thought cheerleading, band, football, student council, and all that stuff came in high school, when it mattered. When did it start counting that my six-year-old son can play peewee football, or my eleven-year-old boy can throw a lacrosse ball? Exploring the sport? Exercising curiosity? Great! But it is not, not, *not* great four times a week. Each of our kids gets one activity. *Uno.* We have three kids ages eleven and under. I'm not aiming for one of them to be the next Mia Hamm; I simply want them to be given the opportunity to discover new things and get some exercise. That's it. The overcommitted kid is another thing this mama doesn't like. Youth is fleeting. I don't want to spend every minute of it on turf, watching my children interact with someone else.

But I promise, I do not, for a single minute, begrudge the mothers who are the room moms, the PTA presidents, the team moms, or the fund-raising chairs. Not only do I not begrudge them their abundant willingness to join everything but I'm willing to bet money that they are better parents than me. That's right, Shirley. I said it. *You are a better parent than me!*

Have I felt the heat of silent judgment on my back as I walk away in these situations? You bet. Have I had to fight the urge to fire back? No question. I love my children. But my time is too precious to invest twenty-five hours in a fundraiser that's going to last four hours and won't matter three months from now. The person to whom things must matter is my child. Always and forever. They are my first calling. Yet I love my mother friends who join and lead and direct. I can't do what they do, and I am proud of them for what they do. I know their hearts are gold, through and through. I admire their many sacrifices. They have chosen their ways to bond with their children. I have chosen mine.

• • • • •

No matter the type of mother we are, nothing we do is ever undertaken lightly. Even if only for a moment, we women always think of the impact our actions will have on our children. It just so happens that I am willing to risk the impact of my son, as a high school student, looking at me in anger and snarling that I never volunteered to fund-raise for his fourth-grade sports team. At which point I will look at him, remind him that I love him, and tell him it's time to go clean his room.

I may have borne a little animosity against other things after having children—things that are not directly related to motherhood but are distasteful because they are its detritus. Note that these things are all a matter of personal preference, but all illustrate how motherhood separates us into camps. Motherhood takes what we were once passionate about and practically injects these things with HGH. Which can make us mean. We categorize ourselves into methods of mothering and the preferences that go with it. This was never a thing I noticed while working full-time. There wasn't a distinction of desire that so immediately and vociferously raised its head once I started working. I didn't wake up one day yelling, "I hate falafels!" the way I one day woke up post-children, and screamed, "If I find one more pair of PJs on the floor I'm going to lose it!"

Motherhood has been hard since the beginning of time, when Eve screamed bloody murder while she was giving birth to Cain and Abel, and later, when they were wrestling and knocking over the skin of goat's milk she'd just filled. And *definitely* when Cain was plotting his brother's death behind his mom's back. I'm sure then Eve was all, *This parenting thing is the pits.*

For me, I discovered I had zero tolerance for things that made my life more difficult. You might be focused on limiting things that make your life more expensive or your days longer. It's all a matter of survival, really. We insulate ourselves from the things that drain us so that we have plenty in the tank for our children, because they will very efficiently deplete our supply. We travel in our own ways to the same destination: the home of that magical creature, the eighteen-year-old child.

I was put off by organic food devotees (You want me to pay double for an apple?), extreme couponing (My house does not have room for eighty-four rolls of toilet paper), mouth breathers (Matt, do you hear me?), and empty boxes left in the cupboard (Noah, the trash can is literally *right there*, next to the cupboard). Little things that required little effort became oddly large preferences. Is it possible to suffer from the wash of pregnancy hormones six years after childbirth? Because I detested these "little" things to the same extent that I was devoted to pickles during pregnancy. Which is a lot.

The separation into camps and the development of preferences that turn into battle lines are almost a ritual of motherhood. We women, strong and fragile creatures from which so much goodness comes, are so perceptive. We see things in ourselves and in each other that men simply cannot see. But this strength has a weak side, and we can make injuries

119

out of nothing. Our own internal wounds can sometimes superimpose intention where there is none, and we can attribute meanness where none exists.

I think we have a tendency to be unkind to other mothers because what we hold as the "right" choice is rooted in a deep, inky well of insecurity. If our method isn't the best, then maybe we've been screwing our kids up the whole time. Maybe *we're* the screwup. The kindest mothers I know are also the most secure. They get it. They don't criticize. They build up. They recognize the difficulty of it all and support instead of tear down. I pray that I'm one of those mothers. If not now, then in the future.

Security in who we are, the security that erases meanness: it's part of this journey we mothers undertake, isn't it? Don't we need to know that what we do isn't the locus of our worth? Our choices in parenting do not make us good or bad. Not even when what we're doing is as meaningful as raising children. Titles and duties, in the long run, don't matter at all.

Last year, a mother made headlines not for what she'd accomplished but for what she'd messed up. Katharine Zaleski, now president of PowerToFly, apologized in a *Fortune* magazine feature for having exercised blatant prejudice against working mothers. Katharine found herself dismissing their ideas, scheduling late-day meetings, and making things intentionally difficult on them, believing they weren't up to corporate par the same way she was as a single woman. Katharine said she had undervalued mothers' contributions because of their responsibilities at home. Now, Katharine is running the first global platform to match women in highly skilled positions with work they can do from home.

Funny how having kids changes things.

Katharine said, "I didn't realize how horrible I'd been—until I had a child of my own. . . . I wish I had known five years ago, as a young, childless manager, that mothers are the people you need on your team. There's a saying that 'if you want something done then ask a busy person to do it.' That's exactly why I like working with mothers now."[3]

Nobody gets to quit motherhood. Even on the impossible days. The answers are elusive and the stakes are high. We love our children the best we can with what we have, and the last thing we need is to be mean to each other in the process.

So high-five, Mama. You're doing a great job.

ten

The Art of War

If you have picked up this book and opened randomly to this page, you will know that I am a mother. *The Art of War* isn't just a centuries-old warfare treatise, it is also my second language. And if you are staring at your little angel flipping through the picture books in Barnes & Noble right now, thinking that this is an overstatement of the few skirmishes you've had with your perfect, towheaded toddler, you've not yet realized that you will be as skilled as Patton by the time that very same toddler graduates from high school. If you are the parent of an only child, it will be warfare between that child and you. If you have more than one child, it will be warfare between them—and also with you. If you have three or more children, it will be warfare between them, with you, and between you and your spouse, because dropping a handful of people in a house together and expecting them to practice "Christlike" love with one another is a great way to feel like you're in a sitcom. (But without the tidy resolutions and studio audience applause.) Three children is apparently critical mass for parenting, and the most stressful number of kids, as indicated by seven thousand American moms in a 2013 survey.[1] Why? Because you've gone from man-to-man to zone defense, and someone's bound to get by you.

In the second century BC, Sun Tzu penned his critical work on military tactics in *The Art of War*. Each of its thirteen chapters describes one aspect of warfare. It is required reading for United States CIA officers, has been used by the KGB, and was extensively studied by the Vietcong during the Vietnam War.

It is this same book that boasts some surprisingly effective maxims for the modern-day mother. For example:

1. *If you know both yourself and your enemy, you can win numerous battles without jeopardy.*

My children are observant. They can read fear, frustration, or anxiety in me like some people read tabloid covers: quickly and judgmentally. Seven o'clock rolls around, and they realize that if I'm more tired than they are, they can ask me for a Pop Tart before bed and I will cave *every time*. And I cave every time because I think if I can just get them into bed by acquiescing to their requests, I will be in a whole different room from them and can close the door behind me when I leave. Like I'm leaving tigers to fight over a slab of meat.

What is the solution here? *Don't buy Pop Tarts, Sarah. Know that you will be tempted by their $1.99 price tag, and while you may think to yourself they are a good purchase, they are most certainly not.* They lack nutritional value. And they will eventually become a source of sugar-fueled rage when your six-year-old finds out that you've hidden them on the top shelf of the pantry to prevent him from stuffing them into his mouth willy-nilly.

And especially don't buy multiple boxes of Pop Tarts, you fool. I just finished getting breakfast for my children who, before I arrived, were clawing their way through the kitchen, tearing open boxes and leaving the freezer open to defrost in their attempt to locate waffles. I realized I had bought four (*why four?*) boxes of Pop Tarts during a trip to the store in which I promised each child they could pick a flavor. Treats are better in small doses. More is never better when it comes to sugar. Unless you're a grandparent and you're going to feed that precious toddler a candy bar the size of his head just before returning him to his mother. (The "spoiling" that grandparents do? Behind their backs we call it "ensuring diabetes.")

Also, if your son has a tendency to get "ticky" and repetitively scream during the course of his video game–playing, do not feed him chocolate milk while he is playing a game on a tablet in the car, on a road trip, in a small space, with four other people, for a long period of time. You will discover too late—nay, when the bottle is empty—that it contained 56 grams of sugar, which is the equivalent of eating three Twinkies full of speed.

I sometimes catch myself looking at my beautiful children and in a shadowy mental lapse, when I am thinking less-than-charming things about them, out slips the thought: *Sweet cheese and rice—was I that annoying to my siblings when I was a child?*

Then I come to my senses and realize that no, that would have been impossible.

I sometimes forget my limits. Like many mothers, I'm prone to pushing myself beyond my comfort zone to do all the things that seem to fall exclusively to mothers. I need to remember that, if I attempt the dentist, the grocery store, the bank, and the post office with three kids on five hours of sleep, when my kids are screaming over the choice of radio station I'm going to find myself screaming at them. Also, the more children you bring to a grocery store, the higher the potential for disaster. This is a universal law. You will inevitably find yourself in the checkout line with three squirming children and a host of grubby little hands reaching for everything at eye level. You will silently curse the store manager for putting things like plastic cell phones and sparkly lip gloss at the same height as your daughter's hands, and she will grab something and look up at you as you're loading your hundreds—hundreds!—of dollars' worth of food on the conveyor belt. You will give up and let her have it, partly because you need to leave this retail nightmare as quickly as possible and partly because you are not fully paying attention to what's being shown to you because you're being bankrupted $4.99 at a time.

Parenting also means knowing your kids well enough to see a conflict coming a mile away. This helps you get a jump on doing the right thing as the situation goes straight to Hades in slow motion right in front of you. Recently, Jesse scrapped with another boy at the football field. It wasn't unprovoked. He had seen the other boy hit a little girl, and Jesse rushed to defend her. Thankfully, my son's thirst for blood is tempered by his chivalry. I thank Matt for both these traits.

"You can't hit a girl!" he howled. And without a further thought, he ran to pick up a plastic noisemaker and whip the other kid like a bass drum. Matt sprinted after him, but rage makes Jesse quicker than the average child.

Oh, shoot, Matt thought as he sprinted. *Here it goes*. And there it went. The kid—let's call him Andy—gave it right back to Jesse, and at least twice in the face. There was a difference of many years between the boys, so Jesse's tears after getting smacked with a bag full of gear may actually have saved him. It seemed Andy stopped the onslaught of his own accord because he felt sorry for Jesse. Jesse, however, was still furious. To his mind, justice had not been served. Plus, now his face hurt.

On the way home, Matt explained to Jesse that Andy's actions were motivated by something other than the typical obnoxiousness of budding testosterone. Matt told Jesse that Andy's heart was broken. As it turned out, Andy's mother was in prison.

Jesse burst into tears. Which was affecting and beautiful and miserable all at the same time, because even when you think you know your children, they will always surprise you. Still sporting crimson welts from his scuffle, Jesse's rage melted to compassion. His little heart was broken for another person.

"I didn't know, Daddy! I didn't know that Andy's mommy was gone!"

So tender is my Jesse that when he walked into my office and began explaining how practice had gone, he didn't get more than a sentence out before he burst into tears yet again. After Matt sat down and explained what I was unable to grasp from Jesse's choked explanation, Jesse turned to me.

"It's gonna be too late to say sowwy when I see him because he won't wemember!"

"Uh, no, Jesse. I think Andy will remember getting hit with a giant purple horn."

But I could barely console him. "Mom, I didn't know his mommy was gone and his heart was hurting. I didn't know!"

This, of course, made *me* cry. Now there were two of us with broken hearts. Jesse, "son to [his] father, still tender, and cherished by [his] mother," was showing tenderness to someone else (Prov. 4:3).

Knowing your children and yourself, observe both. This helps a mother discover how very blessed she is. Because when she is prepared for the expected things she is all the more enthralled by the unexpected ones. Sometimes motherhood's surprises are just miracles by another name. Even at 10:42 p.m., when she's still petting her son's head and praying he'll cut it with the compassion already so she can finally go to bed.

2. *All warfare is based on deception.*

I hate to tell you this, but at some point, your children are going to lie to you.

I know you think this is impossible. I know your family follows God's commands and makes a point to distinguish right from wrong. But lying? It's rooted in self-protection, and your children will soon enough realize that it can get them out of trouble. You will at some point find yourself in a thick hedge of misinformation that your children have no interest in cutting down. This is particularly the case among siblings, who will each work their absolute hardest to shovel the blame onto someone else when your favorite lamp suddenly crashes in the room in which all three have previously been wrestling. You will separate them. You will question them. You will totally Gestapo them, and they will not come clean. They will also be so earnest in their pleas that the truth will be very nearly impossible to discern. They will, as they grow, become so adept at deception that they will even master the body language that accompanies the truth. They will look you dead in the eye and lie their freckled faces off. And then when you discover the lie, you are going to want to freak the freak out, because you will think telling you the truth when you had the decency to cart them around among your innards for nine months is the least they could do.

When I was young, my parents gave me a sweet little book called *Jimmy and the White Lie*. I would like to clarify that I wasn't prone toward some particular mendacity. In fact, I was so self-regulating that if my eyes unintentionally drifted to a classmate's paper during an exam, I would come home and "confess" my failing to my parents. I probably became the book's steward only because my parents didn't have the guts to look at my siblings and tell them outright they were actual liars. *Jimmy and the White Lie* is by a mysterious someone named Bartholomew. I don't know why Bartholomew didn't have a last name. Maybe he thought he'd one day be as big as Prince. Or Cher. One name takes a certain level of confidence and greatness to pull off. (That is why I am quite comfortable with Sarah Parshall Perry. Three names, you see.)

Jimmy was a kid who broke a window during some backyard baseball and then lied to both the home owner and his parents about what had actually happened. This lie is personified as a white, puffy creature that continues to grow larger as the consequences of Jimmy's lie begin spiraling out of control. Eventually, Jimmy can no longer contain the lie and has to fess up because the lie doesn't even fit in his room anymore and comes barreling down the hallway *Ghostbusters* style.

In reality, this doesn't happen frequently enough. Lies don't always grow. Sometimes they're just content to hang out in your child's bedroom and high-five their perpetrators while Mom sweeps up the broken lamp and mutters to herself in the other room.

I have been pleased to find that if I lower my voice and get down to their eye level, reminding my children that they can "tell me anything," they will sometimes, when the sun is in the proper position, fess up. Like Jesse who, when I kept him home from school one day after he complained of a stomachache, was gently petting my arm when he whispered, "Because I don't want to lie anymore, I have to tell you that I'm not really sick." Because he can straight-face a lie like an inmate at Sing Sing. Because he has a singular ability to know when I absolutely have to get something done. And then there was Grace, who in a moment of devoted tenderness and transparency admitted, "I scream to get attention, and sometimes I act like I'm sick when I'm really not."

You will note here the theme of "acting sick" or "being sick" in my children's admissions. One might think this stems from my own autoimmune disease, but in reality it springs from my husband's complete and utter intolerance to pain, discomfort, or illness of any kind. If either of us has to die early, I hope it's me so I don't have to listen to him complain of his gout when he's seventy.

However, deception takes more than one form. Parents sometimes "characterize" things in such a way as to keep the machinery of the day going without major conflict. Consider the following translation guide for parents.

Q: "Mom, when can we go to Disney World?"

A: "When Jesse gets a little older."

Jesse was "older" at three, four, and six. At first it was "When Jesse is out of diapers" or "When Jesse doesn't need an afternoon nap anymore." Then there were no specific developmental milestones to point to, so it was just "When he's older."

Translation: I am putting off this decision as long as possible because I know I am going to have to sell my plasma to be able to afford it, and the thought of four days in the "small world" while waiting in line for chicken fingers makes me want to spork my eye out.

Q: "Is Santa Claus real?" (Noah would always ask this. The younger two took the fat man's existence as a given, but Noah was always looking to break the system by finding a weakness in it like some kind of MI6 operative.)

A: "Well, I don't have any other explanation for the magic of Christmas, do you? Doesn't it seem like he's real?"

Meaning: First, I will divert your attention with a question because I know you love puzzles. I can very easily make all this sound like some magic riddle. Second, I will avoid an outright answer at all costs because I know you wouldn't be able to keep your mouth shut if I were to tell you that I'm the one wrapping, decorating, and laying out presents until 2 a.m. Christmas morning. I know you have a compulsive tendency to torch your siblings' innocence whenever you can. I will not be privy to it, do you hear me? I will *not*! Also, you are only eleven, and as long as you're still in elementary school I'm going to continue perpetrating the fraud of the big elf whenever possible. Between the tooth fairy, the Easter bunny, and that guy, he's the easiest to prove anyway, considering that he shows up in the movies, on TV, and at the mall. Commercialism's got my back, kid.

> Q: "Why did you tell me I could see Claire this weekend, and I didn't? You lied to me!"

> A: "First, don't you take that tone with me, young lady. Second, things changed this weekend and we weren't able to get together with her. I will call her mom about meeting up next weekend, okay? Third, don't take that tone with me, and definitely don't call me a liar."

Translation: I forgot your brother had a lacrosse game and that we were supposed to go out Saturday night, which means I'd have left all that play date nonsense to a babysitter and that was way too much for her to coordinate. Also, Claire lives across town and travel time would have been an hour, round trip, and I'm exhausted, and didn't you just go to a birthday party on Friday night, anyway? Who are you, Paris Hilton?

> Q: "Can we [insert request]?"

> A: "We'll see."

Translation: Probably not. Unless (1) we come into some unexpected money, (2) a twenty-four-hour day suddenly becomes a twenty-seven-hour day, or (3) someone else does it. Maybe we need to call Grannie and see what she's up to.

The deeper questions are the harder ones to answer, and their translations are hard for kids to understand. These answers don't involve deception. Just a mother's willingness to select her words very, very carefully. It is hard work, explaining the unfortunate rules of the world to an eight-year-old who just wants to be pretty and popular and buy everything her heart desires. I am realizing this also sounds a little bit like a grown-up woman I know. Nevertheless, while you may have years' worth of training in the art of negotiation, or possess the unsurpassed ability to defuse an angry client, there's not a fragment of good it's going to do you when you're faced with the questions that matter.

Q: (a) "Why doesn't Aaron like me?" (b) "Why did Nicky call me fat?" (c) "Why do we have to wait for new cleats until Dad gets paid?"

A: (a) "I don't know. I never liked him anyway." (b) "I don't know, but I think Nicky's dealing with some issues of her own." (c) "Go ask your father."

Translations: (a) Not everyone will like you. My heart aches for you, my gentle-hearted son. You will try to make everyone like you, and it will hurt a little every time you can't, especially when you've tried really hard to do everything "right." If you are a natural introvert, as we both are, it will be even harder because your personality will often be misread as distant or uncaring. I know this from personal experience. If they don't love you—which is, sweet child, virtually impossible to believe, even when you are knocking over people's lunch trays at school *on purpose*—then they are not worth your time. (Yes, I found out about the tray incident.) So move on from those who do not see your value. If they don't build you up, if they don't edify your life, they are not intended to be a part of it. Be who you are, the perfect thing God has created you to be. He and I love you so very much, and in time, others will love you too. Even if those "others" are not the ones you're chasing. The ones who will love you are the ones who are supposed to.

(b) Looks don't matter. But it will feel every day like they're supposed to. Unless I can find a way to prevent you from seeing a magazine or watching television ever again, you will probably fight a regular battle as you get older that includes cycles of dieting and exercising or, in my case, just lying on the couch eating peanut butter from a jar while silently loathing the starlets on *Access Hollywood*. Remember this, my strong and beautiful daughter. Carve it on your heart: "For the LORD sees not as man sees: man looks on the outward appearance, but the LORD looks on the heart" (1 Sam. 16:7 ESV). God made you healthy and strong. Your body can do amazing things and was put together in an amazing way. You and I will make sure you're healthy, together. But as for some perceived model of "perfect"? It doesn't exist. In fact, it's always changing. You will never meet it because it's a moving target. Your mother, for example, would have done swimmingly in the Renaissance. Full figure! Pale skin! Light hair! But I haven't gotten around to building my time travel machine, so I'm going to have to make peace with the way I'm put together, here and now. You will too. If not right away, then over time and by learning what things matter and what things don't. You are so beautiful—inside and out. You are so loved, for all that you are.

And just remember: if the skirt says size six but fits like a ten?

You're a size six.

(c) Money doesn't matter. But boy, it sure makes things easier. I will not lie: it feels great to look at your bank account and see commas instead of decimal points. I am just imagining, though. When you're older, I will share with you the many mistakes your father and I have made with money in our lives. You can love money when you have it, and you can love it when you don't. You'll love it by lying in bed at night, thinking, *If I just had a little bit more.* You may at some point feel like you're doing nothing but chasing it. But remember, son, "Keep your life free from love of money, and be content with what you have" (Heb. 13:5 ESV). The simpler and freer of clutter your life is, the easier it will be for you to see the amazing work God is doing in it. Relying on him to provide everything in his perfect timing prevents money from clouding your perspective. And it helps you pursue your work—your career—with abandon, because your worth is not calculated according to a salary. In fact, your worth isn't tied to your work at all.

Finally, my precious child: overdraft protection.

3. *Appear weak when you are strong and strong when you are weak.*

Matt and I are co-commanders in this racket. While he's the "final say" on most of what we do as a unit, I am oftentimes left to my own devices. Particularly when he's traveling.

135

This is where the calamitous use of bribes comes in. Matt's ability to make our kids "toe the line" exceeds mine. I am moved by tears, by wails, by begging. He is not moved at all. Therefore, when he travels, I resort to bribes out of what I believe is necessity but may just in fact be weakness of construct that makes me unable to set limits. I have promised outings, treats, little toys. I have agreed to sleepovers and movies and extra-late bedtimes just to get myself a moment's peace when previous maneuverings have failed. In an effort to shorten the campaign, I sometimes resort to the shortcuts of assured victory. While I am not proud of this, at least I follow through (begrudgingly, and with a promise to myself that it won't happen again). Because I don't want to appear weak . . . er . . . break my word.

The bribe is the last resort. It is the thing you swear off using when you are without child. You will curl your lip at the mother in the zoo gift shop with the crying toddler who wants the $65 stuffed elephant when she promises him ice cream instead as long as he stops crying. You will think to yourself, *Not I. I won't ever use bribes*. You will also swear that you won't feed them Pop Tarts, or let them watch more than thirty minutes of TV a day, or let their rooms get messy. Poppycock! You're going to come to real, intimate terms with what is real and what is ideal after you have a child. And you'll come to terms even quicker if you have more than one.

• • • • •

Speaking of intimate terms, it is at this point I would like to say something about personal space: you will lose it so fast you won't even have time to mourn its loss.

How painful this sacrifice will be depends largely on your level of comfort with physical touch and personal boundaries. It will also depend on the personality of your spouse. If, for example, you chart a life course with someone who is content to host a dinner party in his pajamas, the robbery of your boundaries begins even before your children are born. I am a former ivory-tower dweller who is now an over-sharer. When I got married my life's confines were slaughtered like sacrificial lambs.

So, now you've met my husband.

As for myself, my primary "love language" is physical touch.[2] I wanted to eat my babies up when they were born. I could not bear to put them down and even struggled with offering them up to well-meaning visitors when I was asked if they could be held. Today I still cannot kiss or hug them enough. Jesse scrambles into bed with me every morning. Matt makes a point of waking him thirty minutes early so he can run to my room and get into a bigger, warmer, more comfortable bed with a mother who pulls him in like a blanket under her arm. Grace hugs me around the waist with all her might and kisses me so often I lose track of it during the day. Even my reticent Noah comes to me without being asked and wraps his arms lightly around me, seeming to fear that he will break me. It's for this reason I experience lesser injuries to my sense of dignity and boundaries than most.

But. I have not been able to go to the bathroom in peace since 2004. I have had full conversations with my sons through the bathroom door. These dealings have included notes slipped between the bottom of the door and the tile, knocks and inquiries as to whether I was "done yet," and even fingers—fingers coming from under the door like they do in a horror flick where the zombies signal their presence before they bust through the door with a hatchet.

A traveling husband further corrupts my personal space. During each of his trips, my bed is invaded by middle-of-the-night marauders. They are sometimes loud (Grace and Jesse) and sometimes stealthy as bats with sonar (Noah). If I'm lucky, I wake up in the morning and only then realize that sometime during the night, the covers have been breached. Something about Daddy's absence flushes my children's sleep patterns right down the toilet.

Certain nights I get more than just one extra in my bed. That's really a blast. Not only does my bed not sleep four but there sometimes transpires a fight between the one who has priority based on the fact he or she got there first and the one who comes later. For example, last night Noah arrived first, complaining his ears were itchy. (*What?*) Later it was Jesse, asking if he could sleep with me. When they discovered each other, voices were raised. There's nothing that guarantees my total lack of functionality in the morning better than two kids screaming above my face at 4 a.m.

I solved the mounting crisis by cramming myself in between them. So much love, expressed in this wanting to sleep with me. So much love I want to kick them both onto the floor. (Not really, but kind of.)

The boys also love to stand six inches from my face when talking to me. In fact, they do nearly everything in front of my face. They do things I would rather not see, and the things I've scream-cried at them not to do in public. And they are still the most naked children you will ever meet.

There is also the lap sitting (when I'm trying to type or eat), the toothbrush using (when they have their own toothbrush only a few feet away), and the food eating (when they are served exactly what I am—and usually better, in larger quantity). Oh, the food eating! Jesse will not share his precious food for all the world. He is greedy with his gobbling, and even I (his "favorite") can't get him to surrender a bite of a cookie or a bit of his bagel. But my plate? Fair game. Everyone who walks by picks something off of it. I missed the statute informing all mothers that their food was no longer solely theirs. Maybe I should be more content with hunger pangs. But for the same reason that I am a rotten dieter, people eating off my plate does not please me. I will offer them a bite, if given the chance and if asked nicely. It's the dirty-handed grabbing that fries my hide.

When you have traveled the path from punching a clock to raising a brood, there's a certain adjustment required as you experience the full-on assault of things you once considered sacrosanct: personal space, hot meals, bathroom time. Human dignity, it turns out, is fungible. You will at some point use your shirt to wipe the boogied nose of your six-year-old as the school bus arrives. You will eat an unknown substance or smell something that's wrinkling noses in an effort to get your daughter to stop asking you to "Try this!" You will have full conversations with three children from behind a shower curtain. Until the little one decides he is going to be smart and pull back the curtain.

Kids steal boundaries because they have none.

Part of your strength as a parent in this long campaign comes from understanding what your children are saying. Simple enough, right?

Well, you know how they used code breakers in World War II? How the Allied Forces used symbols and translators and mathematicians to intercept communications, make sense of what was being spoken, and win the war? Yeah. It's like that. Kids have their own way of communicating, and lots can get lost in translation. So you'll need proficiency in code breaking. Maybe it's time for you to pick up Sudoku.

Grace: "Mom, if I don't get the Barbie dream house, I will dieeeeee!"
Oh, so you meant you were just going to stick it in the playroom and let the spiders use it as their personal condo?

Noah: "I totally nailed that math test, Mom!"
Oh, so you meant you actually, literally, failed the test—like, with a huge, red F across the top?

Grace: "Mom! Jacob used both f-words today at school!"
Oh, so you mean he used the totally verboten word, and another "f-word" that is apparently so awful I don't even know what it is?

How about the language that cracks open the mystery of developing minds? How about the stuff that sounds grown-up and childlike in a terrifying combination that leaves you nervously laughing because you realize control of your children is fast becoming elusive, that they exist in a world to which you are not always invited?

Jesse: "Grace, you can't wear that to a street fight."

Noah: "Fine, Grace, you can come with us. But where we're going, you're going to need a torch."

140

Noah: "Grace! You look like you just stepped out of Nicki Minaj's closet. You better go change."

Sometimes, the language of childhood isn't quixotic or mysterious. Sometimes it's direct, and you get to prepare for what's coming. Like when your small child says he has a booger and he's not afraid to use it.

He is, in fact, not afraid to use it.

* * * * *

Easter is one of my favorite holidays. It brings the bright promises of spring and redemption. An end to the winter both literal and spiritual. It means much to us as Christians, but as a mother I also love that it's still such a treat for my children. When I am feeling particularly crafty, I will hang Easter egg ornaments from our tree and tell the children that the bunny brought them while we were sleeping. I will occasionally even leave bunny "footprints" on the stairs.

But the clothes! Oh, the nicely pressed, unsullied Easter clothes that, after fastidious selection, hang untouched in their closets until the morning comes when we prepare for church and I can stand their ungrateful selves on the front porch for some pictures. No one snacks or drinks on the drive to church. I don't care if they have lasagna with Yoo-hoos once they get downstairs for children's church, but we will walk into the house of the Lord looking like we mean it, by George.

This past Easter, our dear pastor was preaching on Christ's sacrifice and his great love for us. It was one of those moments when a sermon was not just a sermon. It was the Lord speaking directly through his servant and into my heart.

141

Even the Easter lilies bent outward like trumpets heralding a miracle. On the way home, I turned to face the kids in the backseat. Noah was trying to take off his tie and had inadvertently bumped Grace in the process, which had led to totally advertent hitting. I put my hand up.

"Guys!"

The hitting stopped (Easter miracle).

"Let's remember what Pastor Mike said today. Christ forgave us, and we ought to forgive each other. Let's try to practice loving each other like Christ loves us. Let's start by saying something kind to one another."

Pause.

"Nice job wearing pants, Noah," Grace sneered.

Noah retorted, "Way to stop smelling, Grace."

So there it was. That combination of half-marvelous, half-irksome, all-child speak that only kids are capable of and only their parents fully understand.

As that carefree professional girl, I excelled at settlement and negotiation. Hating to see adversaries made from everyday failings, I was happy to see each party walk away satisfied. Some days, no one in our house is satisfied. Children do not see reason or common sense. The simplicity of "Say something nice!" can become an exercise in juvenile sarcasm. Though I think I brought that on myself, because I'm sure by now it's clear I love sarcasm.

To children, jumping naked into a frigid pool the second week of April sounds just as good as waiting until June, when they can also wear a swimming suit and not die of hypothermia. There is no concept of future benefit. Theorems such as, "Eat your vegetables because you'll grow up healthy and strong," are lost on them. Your smarty-pants logic is utterly useless. This is a real buzzkill when you actually have a degree that evinces your capability to reason with someone and provide a compelling explanation, backed by evidence, as to why a certain outcome should prevail. Children are creatures of the immediate. I've been able to stretch the concept of behavioral investment out for only a few weeks at a time. Waiting two weeks to buy a video game as a reward for good grades works okay. Telling the kids that we'll go to the beach during summer vacation if they're good in March is practically begging for mutiny.

And here's the value of that: you have to live in the moment. In fact, for the most part, your kids are not going to let you live any other way until they're in high school and you're getting college applications together. Parenting is about immediate action calculated for future benefit. Until that payday, it's all right up in your face, all the skirmishes and the stuff lost in translation. You, the general, will have to calculate the right time for various surrenders. Sometimes the surrenders are to the notion of nothing more than simply surviving. Just getting by. And that's okay. Learning to surrender is a fairly awesome thing.

●　●　●　●　●

In no job other than motherhood does God provide you your own anthropologist: someone with big observations in a little body who sees the simple and important underneath the complicated and difficult. Somehow, and without knowing it, children understand the nature and essence of humankind.

I left Jesse's bedroom the other day when he was in the middle of a white-rage meltdown. Things were thrown. Threats were made. I felt like my ears were bleeding. I told him that when he had calmed himself down he could come out and talk to us. This answer didn't satisfy him. As I turned my back to leave, Jesse screamed after me, "Come back here! You're not done making me feel better yet!" Jesse had cut straight to the core. He had no time for shams. He knew it was a mother's purview to heal a broken heart. He was also manipulative enough to know that this would make me turn on my heel, stifle a grin, and come back to kiss his sweaty, tear-soaked face.

These words were uttered by the same child who, the day before and in the midst of a terse discussion about housing that we probably shouldn't have been having in front of our child, started singing, "He's got the whole world in his hands."

This isn't a song I'd heard him sing before or since. But boy, he understood the conflict and stress between Matt and me. He saw more than we thought he had, as children often do. And as though tapped on the shoulder by the Lord, Jesse was used as a small vehicle to deliver something big and amazing: a reminder that we were not in charge, after all. But that the One who was would work it out.

So when the "victory" of parenting sometimes seems like a lost cause, when you're at your weakest and most vulnerable, when you've caved to bribes, forgotten who you are, or neither of you are speaking the same language, remember, my friend, that you are in charge. Trust yourself, because you're the best kind of sovereign commander: the one who rules with love.

eleven

Survival Instinct

Please don't leave, I think.

I'm watching Matt spread his suitcase out on the bed, prepping for another trip. He's folding dress slacks and work shirts and talking through his meetings as I stand nearby. *Please don't leave me alone with these little people. What if there's some kind of insurrection, and they overtake the house?* I don't say any of this, of course. I just smile with lips squeezed thin as dental floss, my arms crossed.

"Um . . . so, *when* will you be back again?" I lean into "when" like a woman about to fall over. "I mean, you know we're good here. So, just, whenever . . ." It sounds totally casual. In opposite world.

He puts his hand on my shoulder. "I'll be back Friday. You know I hate leaving."

I'm sure he does. But I'm sure he doesn't hate eating a steak dinner in peace while watching SportsCenter and then going to sleep in a bed that doesn't contain a child.

How much would I suck at being a military wife with a husband deployed elsewhere? The answer is epically well. I would suck so well at it that it would look like I had an advanced degree in the subject of sucking. I tip my cap to all the wives and mothers who slog it alone. You are to be commended. It seems to me that, by now, you should have won something.

When Matt leaves, the last thing I am thinking about is the worth of what I'm doing. Rather, I'm thinking about how important it is to just make it to Friday alive.

It wasn't always this way.

I once liked to believe that I would not only manage a heroic parenting interlude in Matt's absence but I'd have the youngest reading and tying his shoes by the time Matt came back. I fantasized about field trips, healthy meals, and early bedtimes. Not only would everyone still be alive when Matt got back but they'd also be well advanced. These fantasies were free, so I spent them freely.

You know what wasn't free? How much money it cost to keep everything under control. Like fast food when you're returning from one kid's whatever-practice and no one's had dinner and they're all ready to barbecue each other in the backseat. So much for making a Crock-Pot meal that would cook all day and could be fed to everyone ahead of time. It also cost money to have a babysitter come in for a few hours when the children were really little so I could get some writing done. I read once that Sylvia Plath, after separating from her husband, poet Ted Hughes, would rise well before dawn and begin her writing at 5:00 a.m. every day before her children woke up. I'd use this as a model except for two things: (1) I'm not a morning person (as established) and (2) we all know how things worked out for Sylvia.

Having lost a paycheck and benefits by giving up my out-of-home job, I found that the value of money changed for me. We'd overhauled everything about our spending and saving. There were painful moments when we realized the extent of what we'd financially sacrificed for me to leave work. It felt like moving to England where suddenly the pound is twice as valuable as the dollar, and you're thinking, *All I want is a sandwich!* but it costs nineteen dollars.

One morning, as I was getting the kids ready for school, Grace and I stood at the bathroom sink while I brushed her hair. On the counter was what was left of my yogurt. Not more than a bite or so. There was also one tissue left in the tissue box. Each item cost approximately one dollar when full—a dollar box of tissues and a dollar container of Greek yogurt. Unfortunately, Grace had shed hair all over the bathroom counter and my yogurt had picked up most of it. Hair in food is a good way to get most anyone retching, so I reached for the last tissue in the box to pick it all up and toss it in the trash without having to touch the hairy dairy. Then I paused for the following calculation: Was the use of the last tissue, costing approximately two cents, worth shielding my gag reflex from the yogurt hair, if there was approximately ten cents worth of yogurt left?

This is what happens when you have kids. Because they do thing like use one-tenth the entirety of a tissue box for a halfhearted nose wipe when you're begging them to stop sniffling and just go blow their nose. Then an hour later you find twenty-three tissues in the trash, some of which haven't been used at all. It makes you want to tear your hair out.

When you have children, you find yourself thinking about things you never anticipated, fearing things you never envisioned, and being mad about things for which you thought you'd have infinite tolerance. Like those Donners, you find yourself scrambling for ways to survive.

●　●　●　●　●

On certain weekends, as is the case in most households, we stuff too much onto the agenda. The Perrys sometimes decide that they're going to take a span of forty-eight hours and catch up on every playdate, couples' dinner, and party we can possibly remember. What we think is the "thriving" of our family actually reverts things to simple survival. We do it to ourselves. Like we've eaten all our food stores two days into a nuclear winter and then complain about being hungry a week later. And sometimes all it takes are eggs made the wrong way to send us right back into the wasteland.

I will eat an egg in any form. I am not picky. Growing up in "America's Dairyland" not only set me up for a potential appearance in "My 600-lb Life" (I've never turned down an entrée with cream) but also gave me ample opportunity to sample all kinds of farm-fresh goodies. I had the misfortune of discovering the hand-churned ice cream in the cafeteria at the University of Wisconsin during my first year of college, and my clothing suffered appropriately. The freshman twenty-five is evidently not a "thing."

But Noah is picky. He prefers his eggs fried, sunny-side up, with enough runny yolk to make a mess of his plate. On this day, Matt started breakfast in the kitchen, and the eggs served at Café Perry were scrambled.

Which naturally should have been my first clue that everything that day was headed down the tubes.

Matt served the eggs with a side of toasted sourdough. Thoughtful of him, I thought. Maybe even cosmopolitan. To Noah, though, it was disgusting, and he weakly stifled a heave when his plate was served. Only moments before, a Minecraft LEGO project over which he had labored for an hour was nearly complete when he pressed too hard on a brick and the whole thing came down.

That's actually how I woke up on this particular morning. Not the creep of sunlight into my room or the buzz of the alarm. No, I heard my ten-year-old losing his mind over LEGO construction gone awry in the bedroom directly below mine.

Noah had also come to the morning breakfast table off one of the most devastating losses of his life. What loss, you ask? His dog? A family member? No. The night before, Noah's beloved Seattle Seahawks had lost to the New England Patriots in the Super Bowl. To make it worse, they'd done so at the one-yard line with seconds left on the clock. And to make it even worse than that, they'd done it when, despite having the best running back in the NFL (Marshawn Lynch), Coach Pete Carroll had decided his quarterback, Russell Wilson, should throw the ball instead. An undrafted Patriots rookie named Malcolm Butler jumped the route and intercepted the ball to deliver the Seahawks the kind of crushing, endgame blow no one thinks possible.

My husband helped me write those last three sentences.

It was, some said, the worst play in NFL history. The wail that came from the TV room downstairs made the hairs on my neck vibrate.

In our house, it was the worst of everything. No, it wasn't just the worst, it was breathtakingly bad. It was slamming and screaming and hitting bad. It was the howl of disappointment that comes from the bottom of your belly bad. It was the inability to distinguish yourself from your favorite sports franchise bad. In Noah's mind he *is* the Seahawks. Their loss was a declaration of his own loser-ness.

Noah came upstairs to the living room where we'd watched the same play and fell to his knees, sobbing.

"I just can't believe they let me down like that!"

The Super Bowl was the crowning event of another over-scheduled weekend. Two birthday parties, one sleepover, soccer practice for Grace, a visit with my parents, a visit to see a sick friend in the hospital, grocery shopping, and dinner out. Seriously. The only place we weren't seen was on the Jumbotron in Times Square.

This is Perry-typical. I am going to tell you I hate it, and might be met with flack once this account is read, but one of us (hint: *not me*) loves chaos. Said person is not discouraged but rather invigorated by it. This is because said person is so used to it. But said person is trying, and is aware of it, and we are working on it together. Because said person is awesome and worth the work. But also, he loves chaos.

In my own way, I appreciate the tension of commitment and have been known to follow suit. But only a little, and only when I am under the gun for a project. I remember distinctly a term paper I had to write in French on the life and works of Victor Hugo. We were given three months to finish it, and I started it the week before it was due. I remember late nights in the library hysterically trying to conjugate the word *create*, so that I could finish. One sparse, tortuous French sentence at a time.

Too much time is actually a bad thing for me. I will find a thousand things to do other than the one thing I'm required to do. I do fairly well under pressure. It's quite possible that I find terror motivating.

But overscheduling and fear don't, as a rule, help your children succeed in real life let alone manage a whole season's worth of disappointment. No, chaos and pressure make our children feel as though they've had every available nerve plucked. It scrambles their brains.

On Monday morning, the eggs, Noah's nerves, our hearts that ached for him, the LEGOs. All scrambled.

Matt turned to me in the living room.

"Do you think we should keep him home from school today?"

Notwithstanding the fact that Matt has called school "government-subsidized babysitting" (this is a joke and he really does love you, teacher friends!), he told me Noah needed the time off. Matt explained, "There's nowhere to go for him today but down. We have to give him a chance to collect himself."

I hated the thought of keeping him home on a "not sick" sick day, but Matt was right.

I told Noah quietly in the other room that Daddy and I had decided to give him a "mental health day."

My darling child burst into tears for sheer gratitude.

"Thank you, thank you so much," he choked.

The wisdom to keep Noah home from school came from God; it helped us give to Noah generously the thing he clearly needed (see James 1:5). There was an unexpected value in the loss of Noah's team. Their losing made *him* lose it. In turn, we saw something we originally hadn't—that our attempts at thriving, our trying too hard for too much, had sent us back into survival mode. We had to regroup.

Noah spent the day reading in his room, playing the Playstation, eating lunch with me, and asking if he could help with anything. And then we laid on my bed and watched the movie *Bridge to Terabithia*—a favorite book of both of ours—while he held my hand.

They say you can't unbreak an egg. But I guess you can unscramble it. When you figure out how much is too much and you're back to the basics on motherhood's journey, then you can move cautiously past survival. One loss, one breakfast, one gain at a time.

•　•　•　•　•

It was February, and I was on the way to Patient First in the middle of an ice storm with Grace in the backseat. This is never how a good story starts, by the way. Unless Ed McMahon is waiting for you at Patient First with a giant check and a bouquet of balloons, nothing good can come of a visit to Patient First. They practically scream, "I waited too long, and now the pediatrician's office is closed." Which was the case.

A week and a half prior, Grace and I had been headed to the barn for her riding lesson. In her haste, Grace had slipped on a patch of black ice in front of our house and skinned her knee, tearing through her breeches and setting off a little avalanche of blood.

I gasped. "Ooh, Grace! We have to run back in the house and patch that up!"

"No!" she howled. "We're already late! Let's just go."

This was a critical decision but the wrong one. It was wrong for two reasons. First, I had let an eight-year-old act as final authority between the two of us, particularly on a matter of health and welfare. Second, I didn't just grab a spare pair of breeches before heading into an environment that was seething with foreign bacteria. Forty-five minutes later, my daughter was consequently kneeling near/around/possibly in manure as I chatted with the trainer and assembled her equipment.

A week later, her gashed knee wasn't healing.

Well, duh.

I was washing and patching and applying Neosporin. But the wound got redder, and hotter, and finally full of pus. Which is when I sent a picture to my mother.

I would like to pause here to thank God and people way smarter than me for the development of the smartphone. Even when you've been a parent for eleven years, you may find yourself telling your child to hold still so you can get a good shot of some weird bump on their lip. My mother's been able to call everything from incoming molars to fever blisters via smartphone, which she would tell you is a function of having had a nurse for a mother, and I would tell you is a function of the fact that she watches way too much Discovery Health channel. In either event, she told me it was probably a staph infection and I was going to need to get it looked at.

I told Matt. As is typical for him, he downplayed the idea of something "bad" so hard he was practically digging it a grave. This is a defense mechanism I don't think he knows I see in him. Of course, now he's going to read this book, and that's that. When things are hard, as they have been for us (in weird, repetitive, pile-on chunks), I think Matt likes to tell people that it's "nothing" because he's terrified it's actually "something," and he thinks this somehow makes him better prepared to deal with it. He does this in the same way that I anticipate the worst possible outcome when I really want something, because I feel like it prepares me for disappointment.

This is actually the first time I've thought about us doing the exact same thing: he prepares for the best outcome while being afraid of the worst; I prepare for the worst outcome while hoping for the best. These are our survival instincts, and it turns out they are both crap. But at least we can say that, after a decade and a half together, we end up somewhere in the middle. It's a weird way to find balance. We're clearly perfect for each other.

Two days and a half teaspoon of pus later (ok, yes, this is *approximate*), I croaked, "That's it! I'm taking her to Patient First!" This line-drawing-in-the-sand came on a Saturday after our pediatrician was on his way to Bermuda or something, and so I had to go to the quickie-doc. In an ice storm. On a Saturday. By the time we were finally seen, it was late afternoon. I may have come on a bit too strong for the doctor. I explained what had happened and then peeled off the bandage.

"I think it's a staph infection," I said.

I find that doctors generally don't care what you think it is. That is because your fifteen minutes on WebMD is allegedly no match for their eighteen years of schooling. Allegedly.

The doctor didn't say anything but made some notes in the computer while chatting with Grace. I may as well have been a box of rubber gloves for all the attention he gave me. He ignored my statement and continued his computer notations. I started to get agitated and tried to ask politely what he thought of the oozing wound on my daughter's knee.

"Well, you know she just probably got some dirt in it and it's irritated. You can keep up with the Neosporin."

He was still typing. He had yet to turn around. I was getting antsy.

"Excuse me, doctor," I interjected, "isn't staph *bacteria*? I mean, we've been rinsing and changing bandages and using Neosporin for nearly ten days. It's getting worse."

This must have shaken him out of his self-impressed reverie, because he finally turned around.

"Well, yes . . . I suppose it could be staph too. I mean, staph can be found all over, and it can get in wounds—"

"Which would make them hot, red, and ooze pus? Which would prevent them from healing and actually cause them to get worse over time?"

Which is when he pulled out a prescription pad and wrote Grace a prescription for Cefazolin.

You know what surviving does? Surviving helps you realize the value of your own spine when you're used to second-guessing your own decisions and folding in half when someone tells you the opposite of what you suspect is true. They call it "woman's intuition" for a reason. They also call it "mother's instinct." I call it "possible hysteria," but so what? I'll let you think I'm overacting because I'd rather be wrong and look like a fool than be proven right and deeply regret not speaking up earlier.

On that icy Saturday, another of motherhood's truths revealed itself. Surviving parenting meant believing in myself. It meant boldness and inner resolve. I had to accept that I was capable and act like it. Because it wasn't just me needing to be intrepid for myself for the chance of a raise or a promotion; for the setting of limits or self-defense in the face of contrarian colleagues. It was no longer me, for my own sake, cringing at the heckling of a student or hiding in the parking garage when someone called me a nasty name. When you have children, the confines of your courage will be under constant stress. Every day requires boldness of varying degrees. But the value of their needing you? Of being the person on whom they rely for their protection?

It helps you value yourself too.

•   •   •   •   •

Breaking from parenting's ever-present hard work is essential. I've found it's possible to dreamily stroll the frozen foods section with a cup of coffee and feel downright euphoric when you get a few minutes to yourself. I have learned to invest in my own personal account and step outside the fray occasionally so that I can come back to my family a better mother and a better spouse, so that I can teach them the value of taking care of themselves in order to take better care of others. See, prisoners make shivs out of soap bars because they never get to leave the compound. I have heeded this as a warning to get out of the house on occasion. Which brings me to two more keys to survival.

Namely: (1) don't get involved in a car crash and (2) make time to stop and smell the manure.

I was on the way to the barn yesterday. The barn outing was the last segment of a very full day. I was in full single-parent ops mode with Matt on the road. But I was so exhausted I'd slept through my alarm, an alarm dubbed "radar" by the good people at Apple. There are other alarms on my phone from which I cannot choose because I will sleep right through them. Alarms called "silk," "by the seaside," or "twinkle."

These are probably better for people with heart issues who will hit cardiac arrest with an alarm like "radar." "Radar" is the sound I imagine a pilot hears when the dashboard in the cockpit is telling him that the plane is going down. I slept through "radar" yesterday because I was so tired I felt like my bones were melting out of my skin and into the mattress. I had exactly twenty minutes to get the kids to school. I managed to get teeth brushed, vitamins administered, bags packed, and kids out the door in nineteen minutes, with a five-minute window before the school bell rang. I gloated all the way back home.

However, as our landlords were in the process of prepping for an impending open house in a few days, they were all over the house. In the yard, on the roof, in the basement. I attempted writing while in the fishbowl of observation. By the way, I understand now why people go on "writer's retreats." You'd think that writing about your own life would be the easiest possible venture, but let me tell you, when four out of the five of you are convinced you are going to get it done but never give you the time to do it, you start thinking about a suite at the Ritz to get away from people. People you adore but who make you crazy with the interruptions. Plus, room service.

While maneuvering around my houseguests, I balanced the checkbook, did a few loads of laundry, ran the vacuum, and packed for the barn. I was prepping for a horse show the next day. Now, you may be thinking this is a ridiculous addition of unnecessary hardship in an already overfull life. You are probably right. But this horse show was part of something that is important for reasons I will discuss in a moment. I had to pack cleaning rags and leather oil. I toted equipment and a list of things to load in the trailer. And I was taking the kids to the barn with me because I didn't have a sitter. This required snacks, tablets, books, and other sundries designed to occupy them while I prepped my horse and my things for the next day. There is *so much leather* involved in the sport of competitive jumping, and it all has to be cleaned.

I picked Noah, Grace, and Jesse up from school and squeezed them under my arms in a tight embrace. My having missed them so much was particularly notable on this day because two of them had been fighting over my face—*yet again*—in the predawn hours as they attempted to squeeze into the same space on the bed. It's a wonder I wanted to see them at all.

See? Motherhood love is a crazy, sacrificial, eat-you-up kind of love.

As we began the thirty-minute drive, I rolled down the windows and passed out snacks and treats. We laughed. We sang at full volume to the songs on the radio. Then we approached a stoplight five minutes from our destination, at an intersection monitored by a red-light camera. We reached it in heavy traffic, at a crawl, when Jesse said something from the backseat and I looked up into my rearview mirror. For a split second. A split second was enough time to rear-end the car in front of me.

Thanks be to God, we were all buckled. The airbags didn't deploy. No one was hurt. There weren't even any spills. We weren't hit from behind, and no one was hit in front of the car directly in front of us. All the other driver got was a dent to her hatchback. So small. Practically minuscule. My Honda, on the other hand, folded like a card table. We couldn't even open the passenger-side door. Radiator fluid was oozing onto the asphalt and the grill was crushed.

"We were in an accident! We were in an accident! We were in an accident!" Noah yelled repeatedly next to me.

I spun around to look at the kids and put my hand on Noah's.

"Is everyone ok? Are you hurting anywhere? Everybody talk to me!"

They were fine. Jesse barely looked up from his iPad to answer me. Apparently, Honda does this thing where they design certain models to crumple like paper so as to absorb impact. I learned this *after* the accident. While surfing the internet for things like "lawsuit against Honda Corporation following collision."

After starting the wheels in motion with the state police and calling my insurance company, I got out to talk to the woman in front of me. Blessedly, she was alone. There were no other passengers to experience my idiot driving. I tapped on her window, and she rolled it down.

"Are you ok? Are you hurt at all? I have the police coming." She turned to me with her little mouse-face and said in a meek voice, "I'm a little shaken up." Tears welled in her eyes.

I told her I'm sure she was and that it was a terrible inconvenience and I wanted to make sure she was ok. I told her I knew how scary this was and asked if she needed me to call anyone for her. We exchanged some insurance information, and as we did she said, "We are supposed to be going to Disney World tomorrow."

Oh no.

"Oh, wow . . . I . . . That sounds wonderful. Well, hopefully this won't interfere with any of that. My kids are in the car with me, and I understand what it's like to keep promises

to your children. I'm sure you're looking forward to that . . .
I'm so very sorry about all of this."

Words were just pouring out of my mouth. When I am
nervous, I talk. A lot. There was so little damage to her car, it
was obvious she'd be able to drive it home. But it was a heck
of a way to start a family vacation. My own overcommitment,
self-imposed, had imposed itself on someone else, and I felt
awful. I had been doing too much and trying to do it all too
fast. I was cramming everything into the tight boundaries of
a few hours. This is a recipe for the hellish devolution of a
perfectly good day, and my proficiency in this regard knows
no bounds. When I was working and childless? Really, the
only person I stood to inconvenience and exhaust was myself.
If I wore myself out, it didn't matter nearly as much as it
did this day, when I pushed my kids to their limits too. My
children were afraid, and I was the one to cause their fear.
I was choked with guilt. Matt showed up ten minutes later,
because as the Lord would have it his plane had landed early
and he was already headed to the barn to meet up with us.
When he arrived, I burst into tears on his shoulder.

I had messed everybody up. The passenger in the other car,
the kids, Matt. Now we required a rental car, an exchange of
vehicles, a body shop, and an insurance adjuster. The perfect
syncopation of a day I'd planned down to the last minute
was shot to you-know-where. There wasn't a single person
to blame but myself.

I was trying to survive in Matt's absence, believing that
the faster I worked and the harder I tried, the quicker I would
get everything done and the sooner I could relax. Life does
not work this way. I could have sacrificed something self-
imposed. I could have pared down our commitments, and

everyone would have been better off. Like the laundry, which has no deadline. (Unless the basket has cracked under the weight of the clothes you have continued to pile in it, and they are spilling out into the hallway. Which isn't as much a deadline as a suggestion that you need to buy more laundry baskets. Which I have done.)

So, a lesson: don't get involved in a car crash because you are trying to do too much and rushing to fit it all in. It is better to do a few things well than do a lot of things poorly. I knew I was frazzled with the kids in the car, and despite our great exchanges and laughter I felt like I was on the clock. Mind-set is essential to survival. I find now as a mother that the faster I move, the less careful I become. I have to make time to stop and smell the manure.

You see, manure comes from horses. Horses are my "thing." I have a girlfriend who runs competitively, another who bakes, and a third who has taken up photography. A "thing" for every mother is of extensive and lasting benefit, though it may be initially hard to conceive. We mothers are prone to a certain insidious form of guilt that doesn't plague those without uteruses of the "used" variety. Horses are the thing I do for myself, the pursuit that fills my bucket so that I can pour what I have into other people.

●　●　●　●　●

I was, as many little girls are, obsessed with horses. Horse posters, horse models, and horse books filled my shelves. I drew horses. I dreamt of horses. There was a short stint with riding lessons. There was no discernable riding talent. And we were a single-income family (my mother having given up her teaching job to stay at home with me and my three siblings). Single-income families don't generally have the means to support an expensive riding habit unless one of them has invented the internet. I shook my fist at the heavens and swore that I would ride again someday.

When I started working as an attorney in Baltimore, I picked up the pastime again. That was many years ago. You would think that many years of practice at something would assure its proficiency. But I can be remarkably bad at it. I am a contradictory combination of control freak and adrenaline junkie. This is the worst possible combination for the pursuit of horse jumping, and my trainer knows it. But she never says anything about it, because she is a good person and I continue to pay her. Also, I have a really good horse. He is not just big and handsome; he also jumps beautifully. An added benefit? He doesn't stop even when I pretty much stand up in the stirrups or get bobbled off the side of his neck after a jump because I haven't been focusing the way I should, or I've grabbed the reins in an attempt to force him to slow down when really what he needs to do is speed up. Control freak plus adrenaline junkie equals my trainer dying a little inside after every lesson.

Without children, I had a life easily crafted around my own interests and self-care. I got regular haircuts and manicures. My toenails did not look like eagle talons. I replaced worn-out clothes. I went out to dinner, to movies, on dates. It is second nature to be self-oriented when there are not knee-high humans clamoring for basics like food.

But it is essential to make time for oneself when the little people come. Yes, "essential."

I attempted "me time" early in parenthood but was overcome with culpability that sucked the joy right out of something as simple as going to the grocery store by myself and leaving the baby with a sitter. This guilt is unnecessary. I have learned that part of this parenting thing is working on yourself so that you can help your children learn how to work on themselves too. I encourage my children's passions. I encourage their exploration. They explore a lot. Soccer, saxophone, gymnastics, lacrosse, football. I actually wish sometimes they'd just stick with something so I can stop dragging my sorry self to Dick's Sporting Goods to try to find all kinds of nonsense like a "pocket girdle."

Though sometimes? This exploration leads to unexpected benefits.

During long days, I carted Grace to the barn with me when Matt and I divided up the kids in an effort to lessen each other's loads. She is an animal lover by nature. Also, by nature, she loves time away from her brothers.

Grace watched everything and asked lots of questions.

"What is that thing in Stuart's mouth?"

"It's the bit, honey. There are lots of different kinds, in different shapes and sizes. It helps guide the horse."

"How high will you jump today?"

"Only as high as Ms. Laura lets me. We will see how Stuart does."

"Why does Ms. Laura yell sometimes in your lesson?"

"Probably because she is afraid I'm going to kill myself."

After the first year, Grace started asking if she could ride too. She was fearful, but her desire to ride overcame it. She insisted she ride the smallest pony in the barn and that the trainer stay by her shoulder at all times. But she did it. Not at my insistence, or anyone else's, but because she wanted to. Grace overcame her fear without anyone's help, other than a lot of silent prayer on my part that she wouldn't nose-dive into the gravel. That was a year ago. Now my young daughter is jumping fences on her own and asking when her next horse show is. "Me" time has turned into "Grace and me" time. I still get to ride by myself most days, and this fills my bucket. But my daughter and I now get to spend summer Saturdays together, side by side with a horse and a pony, watching the other riders and eating pit beef sandwiches in the sun. We smell of earth and manure, and Grace has too many slushies, and she plays with our trainer's Jack Russell, a little wind-up toy of a dog that goes perfectly with ponies and little girls. These are fairly perfect days.

This time with horses not only gives me the time and space to mentally refuel and be a better mother on my return but also teaches me about parenting. I have watched my daughter become brave. I have encouraged her courage and let her fly. I've even watched her fall. This stops my heart every time. I've skidded into the dusty ring next to her and held her hand as she cried, and have performed unqualified neurological exams. But every time, without my prodding, my strong daughter has mounted again and ridden on. Burgeoning boldness in a child is the precursor to perseverance in later life, perseverance that leads to character and hope (see Rom. 5:3–5). Riding and falling and riding again reminds her she can do anything with her Father's help.

Riding also teaches me to trust, something at which I do not excel. This sport requires a point at which the rider must release her grip. It's literally called the "release." As the horse arcs high into the air, the rider has to let the reins go slack enough that the horse can stretch out its neck and make the best effort possible. In the same way, I trust God with my children. He sees the obstacles I cannot and the best way to overcome them. These are his children, after all. And so the parallels between my sport and my children are numerous and humorous. For example, smelling like manure reminds me of how often this mothering job requires dealing with poop.

* * * * *

Sometimes I *sono sola*—I stand alone. Sometimes I also have occasion to use that mostly impractical Latin I have rattling around in my brain. Sometimes pulling the parenting load singlehandedly is hard, and my guess is that military wives and single mothers use certain methods to survive. One of them is family, though I have none anywhere close. So as a substitute, I employ certain tactics in Matt's absence. One of them is to neglect the filth. On any given day, a single square foot of kitchen floor space may boast a half-eaten pepperoni slice, a red Lite-Brite peg, bits of gravel, dog hair, and crumbs from lunch.

Realizing that there is no other grown-up in the house to appreciate it, I let certain things slide when Matt's gone. Because really, how many times can you clean your son's pee off the bathroom floor in the course of a day? The answer is three. You can do it three times before you start to feel like the not-fairytale version of Cinderella and realize no one is coming to give you a fancy dress and take you to the castle. Therefore, I have decided that zero times is better than three times. And guess what? The world keeps on turning. The world will not end because of your dirty house. And you can clean it later when Daddy is back and he's taken the kids elsewhere.

Now, we don't totally descend into squalor. Daily things are done: dishes, laundry, beds made. But the hardest part is actually letting my kids pitch in. Letting your children help is actually one of the quickest ways to determine if you're a control freak. It is much, much easier to do it myself and do it right the first time than it is to stand over an eight-year-old and show her how she ought to hang the shirts in her closet. And it takes *twice as long*. First there are the initial screams of protest. Then there is the carrying of the laundry to the room. Next there is the gathering of empty hangers and the instruction on how to hang. Then there is the picking of half of it back up off the floor, because it all looks like a blind person has hung it with a rake.

Likewise essential to survival: buy the best washing machine you can afford, and preferably also a dryer with some kind of "wrinkle prevention" setting. Because you will tell yourself that you will get around to ironing and steaming mounds of clothes, and at some point you may. This impulse will eventually fade unless, for example, your child is going to be photographed for school pictures or stand front and center for his solo in the spring concert, where all the other mothers will be judging you based on what he's wearing.

Motherhood benefits from increased volume. Not just from industrial washing machines or warehouse club memberships. Take the matter of your car. You can kiss your Civic or your Saturn goodbye if it seats less than six. Sure, it's zippy and fun to drive. But you will get about two weeks into your three children lined up like dominoes in the backseat before someone's head explodes from the screaming. You'll have to cave and get some kind of massive people mover, which will not be fun to drive and whose weekly fill-up will roughly equal the gross domestic product of Swaziland. But this car will be necessary for both your kids and their many accoutrements for whatever sport/party/sleepover/camping excursion they've set you on.

Plus, there are moments when you're also going to have to transport their friends too, which is double mayhem in a small car, particularly because the window seat is always preferred and your car has only so many windows. Your big car will always be dirty unless you pay two hundred dollars to have it regularly detailed, because bigger cars have more room for fingerprints and stale french fries.

And on the subject of volume, no one will be honest with you about the fact that your husband will count as an extra child. I got married and had a six-foot-one baby on the same day. He will be (almost) as messy as the kids. He may leave his giant, boat-sized shoes all over the house to be tripped on. He will not empty his suitcase after business trips. He will pile nine bottles and tubes on the bathroom sink and never put them away, which will surprise you, because it takes him all of ten minutes to prepare himself so what exactly is he using all of those bottles for? He will put his glasses right next to his glasses case and yet not put them inside. Then you will do it for him and he will wail that he can't find his glasses. The toilet paper will always be installed the wrong way, the washing machine will not have been touched by his giant hands, and his illnesses will be the second coming of the plague. He will moan and twitch like he's lying on a pallet of fiery coals, and you will have to force him to do grown-up things to get better, like taking an aspirin or pushing fluids. He will constantly ask you things like, "Am I running a fever?" in his most pathetic voice, and he will tell the kids not to bother him because he is "really, really sick." You will have no choice but to let the kids bother you when *you* are sick, because there is some unwritten rule that a sick mother is still a fully functioning one, whereas a sick father is pretty much dead. When something like the stomach flu ravages your house, you will still have to strip the sheets and spray Lysol while you are holding back your own barf, because who else is going to make sure that everyone gets better? You will, that's who. Because being a mother is not something you can quit.

• • • • •

Most days, though, scattered in between the work of motherhood and its repetitions, the magic of it will peek out at you from in between the mundane. When you sprinkle "reindeer food" made from oats and glitter on the lawn at Christmas. When your children burst into the house calling first for you above all others. When you have your youngest to yourself because your older children are gone for the day, and he leans over and whispers in his still-baby speak against your ear, "I'm so lucky to have such a good mommy."

Pow. Straight to the feels.

Then the magic will straight-up blindside you when you realize the leprechaun was supposed to leave something on St. Patrick's Day and is about to make a mess of longstanding tradition. Because the leprechaun is busy and thought everyone was past the leprechaun stage anyway. Because even Santa now gets the Spanish Inquisition.

Last year, in the middle of the chaos that is so often just a synonym for "us," I was going to let St. Patrick's Day slide. It was a minor holiday; who would notice? They all noticed, and the day before St. Patrick's Day they all asked me—every last one of them, independently, like they were all in on some Dan Brown–level conspiracy—whether the leprechaun was going to come and whether we were going to put out something gold to try to catch him.

It was 4:53 p.m. on a Monday. I had dinner simmering on the stove and homework was spread on the table. The dogs needed to be fed and lacrosse practice was coming up. I bit the inside of my cheek just enough to prevent me from saying something stupid.

"Well, I guess I didn't think about that. Does anyone remember where we put our trap?" Our "trap" is a coupon box set on its side, propped open with a straw, and baited with a shiny game token. Of course they remembered.

Jesse piped up: "I wonder if he will leave us a note like last year!"

Whereupon my brain started to melt. Because this note has traditionally been an elaborate limerick designed to entertain the kids and explain why the leprechaun can't be caught. Their disappointment at a near-miss is tempered by candy or bubbles, something little to entertain them and perpetuate the idea of things enchanting and nearly true.

I looked at Matt in desperation.

"Um, honey, I think you should take all three kids to practice tonight. I think it would do them some good to run around." I made a gesture behind Noah's head of writing with a pen, hoping he would get that I was telling him I had to write the magic letter.

He did not. I tried again.

"They need some exercise, Matt. I'll get out the leprechaun trap while you're gone."

My eyes were wide, and my mouth was a tight bow of frustration.

"Oh, ok," he said. "Let's pack it up, guys."

Ten minutes later, after cleaning up the dinner dishes and making the lunches and coffee for the next day, I threw my purse in the car and sped to Dollar General. I would like to tell you that I was not speeding, but that would be a lie. It's not that I have a permanent lead foot, it's that I'm just permanently anxious. I therefore happen to drive permanently fast.

I grabbed bubbles, St. Patrick's Day cookie pops, and stickers. On the way home, I began to compose a letter in my head, and in the twenty minutes that remained before everyone came tumbling back in the door, I wrote the following:

> March 17 in the year of our Lord, 2015
> I've paid you a visit and taken no gold.
> For none I could find to steal or to hold.
> So I took me some silver from places downstairs,
> Stuffed it deep in my sack to take to my lair.
> But as always, I left you three something behind,
> Because you're good children, despite all the cryin'.
> Treats red, green, and blue to brighten your day,
> But you'll never catch me, no, not to this day.
> So stick out your traps, your contraptions, your boxes,
> I'm cleverer, always, than 10,000 foxes.
> I'm faster of foot than a racehorse or hare,
> So next time, try trappin' me then . . .
> . . . if you dare!
>
> Signed,
> Shamus O'Flannery, resident of County Offlay,
>   Ireland,
> under the bridge, to the right of the river

I printed the letter and decorated it with hand-drawn shamrocks and rainbows. When I heard the car doors slam and the kids came tumbling through the front door, I slipped it into my desk drawer and went to meet them in the kitchen. After they were showered, fed their snacks, and stuffed into bed, I set everything out and collapsed.

"Do you think the letter's okay?" I pleaded with Matt. "I wrote it superfast."

"Mmm?" Matt mumbled, his face half buried in his tablet.

"The letter."

"Oh, yes. No, it's good. You did a really good job." He smiled at me and went back to his tablet.

I've felt the crush of real pressure at work. I've occasionally cut deadlines close, and in moments of mental dusk forgotten meetings or appointments. Yet not once has the prospect of disappointing a boss imbued me with the kind of terror that disappointing my children has. I have sat bolt upright in bed at 2:00 a.m. when I realized I forgot to move the Elf on the Shelf. I have called my mother in a panic and asked her to ship the gift Jesse wants for his birthday to her house instead of mine so it will be there in time. I have, after laying out a bonanza of gifts from "Santa," sat down at midnight to write a letter full of clever rhymes and instructions for the kids to follow before they can get to the presents on Christmas day.

Every year, I fight the urge to write, "Merry Christmas. You can open anything you want as long as you let your parents sleep."

This is another way in which the job of motherhood can be bewildering. The prospect of getting canned is scary. You may be passed over for a raise or a promotion if your performance lacks. There is an obvious action/reaction apotheosis in corporate America. But inferior parenting, forgetting or failing at important things, is terrifying not only for what it means in the present (Will they cry? Will they be angry? Will they ask me one hundred questions to which I don't have an answer?) but also for what it means in the future. There is a real possibility that your children will grow to resent something as adults that you screwed up when they were kids. More disconcerting, there is a possibility that you will forgo the fleeting moment of pure ecstasy that illuminates the face of your six-year-old when he runs to the kitchen and finds bubbles, cake pops, and stickers from a leprechaun.

It will fade, though, when he says, "Bubbles? Bubbles are dumb. We have enough bubbles already. I thought the leprechaun knew that."

Like your boss's, your son's critiques have their place too, I suppose. They certainly keep Shamus O'Flannery from getting too big for his little buckled boots.

twelve

I Feel Bad about My Brain

(And I'm Not Crazy about My Body, Either)

On January 14, 2014, I cried while reading Facebook.

Not for any important reason. I cried because I was reading *The Paris Review*—a literary magazine I follow—and included that day was an interview with Umberto Eco. My first thought was, *Wait a minute, who is Umberto Eco again? Where has my brain gone? Wait . . . what about Joyce Carol Oates? She wrote something, right? I used to know things! It's gone! All gone!*

You will note that this date is relatively recent, and that I, myself, am writing a book, and that reading books is kind of essential to this profession. So I promise to read more of Umberto Eco before my next book. For both of us.

As I scanned the article, I noticed that Eco professed to have some fifty thousand books in his personal collection.[1] Instead of erudite musings on what could be learned from those fifty thousand books, and what subjects were covered in those books, and how long it took a man of his literary stature to achieve such a collection, I wanted to ask Eco if he had ever relinquished his high-minded literary pursuits to be with small children for any length of time. Because if he had? Then, no. I think there's a mathematical formula relevant here, to wit: literary prodigiousness (LP) equals total minutes (TM) minus minutes with children (MC) divided by minutes for book shopping (BS) times rate of brain melt (BM).

$$LP = (TM - MC) \div BS \times BM = \text{brain death imminent}$$

Also, because what my mother said, that "I can't have anything nice with kids around," is one of the truest things uttered, I can fairly guarantee that some of those lovely old books would be covered in crayon or missing pages. (By the way, Umberto Eco is an Italian essayist, philosopher, literary critic, and novelist. He's best known for his 1980 historical mystery novel, *The Name of the Rose*. You're welcome. And thank you, Wikipedia.)

I am a woman in her forties who is still paying off student loans. I burn with the indignity of paying off money I borrowed more than fifteen years ago while feeling like I may as well have just set it on fire. I know I am just passing through, here. I know my education was not in vain and that I am in a temporary place to which God has called me. I know I am doing the most important thing I will ever do and that it must be done now. But when I remember more of "Austin and Ally" than I do the legal concept of "accord and satisfaction," I usually benefit from a reminder.

I avoided "baby" talk once my kids started walking. Matt and I wanted our kids to be better readers and writers, so we avoided the hyena screeching that some people use with toddlers and spoke to them as though they were adults. Our children developed advanced vocabularies. They've never suffered from an inability to communicate. Literal terminology and grown-up phrasing coming from a toddler mouth was adorable—until someone whose name I will not mention but rhymes with "Pat" decided to use hospital-grade medical terminology for body parts. That was not only *not* adorable, it was terrifying. Particularly because these words came out of those little mouths at the most inopportune moments. Like when my girlfriends asked me why their children were suddenly sounding like little Kinseys at school, and were pointing their fingers at their friends who were *raised in a Christian household* and should not have been using certain words, let alone teaching them to other kids. As if children needed any kind of an excuse to be more interested in their "equipment." There's no need to give them the ammunition to tell their friends what the thing is called that "Daddy and me have underneath our clothes." Twenty-four months old is all kinds of early when it comes to sex education. Do yourself a favor and call it a "parrot" or a "transmission." Otherwise, you're in for a conversation like the one I had with a five-year-old Jesse.

Jesse: "All people have penises."

Me (biting the inside of my cheek to keep from laughing, and also thinking that if I were a feminist, I would be through the roof at this, because why would all people have penises but not vaginas?): "No, honey," (scanning the vicinity for Matt, who really ought to be countering this incorrect biological conclusion because it was his fault in the first place the word was even being uttered) "all men do."

Jesse (after a moment's pause for thought): "Well, not all men, actually. Some men have penises that have been cut off. Because of accidents."

So this is the kind of stuff I talk about, now. I find my brain is sometimes stuck in idle. I say a lot of the same things. Sometimes because the kids don't listen. Sometimes because I forget I've already said it. Work offered me a changing landscape. There were new projects and new goals to meet. There were different employees, and clients coming and going, and inventory, and contracts, and a fiscal year. All of it was a whetstone for mental acuity. Motherhood, though? It can look the same day after day. The horizon doesn't change much, and when it does, it seems to do so at a sloth's pace. Sometimes it doesn't even feel like we're moving. Not until the routine is broken because the kids are grown. When we look around us and realize the house is empty and our children have become adults. When we are caught off guard by motherhood, again.

Here is a sample of dialogue from my previous life:

1. "Brian, I'm going to have that request for proposal ready for you next week, but I need the anticipated media spend before I send it."

2. "Steve, I don't think paragraph five of the summary judgment memorandum needs a discussion of defendant's negligence, because we've discussed it in the previous paragraph."
3. "Class, today we're going to be discussing government regulation of the private sector."

Here is today's sample dialogue:

1. "Jesse, don't you *dare* tinkle in the pool again!"
2. "Grace, go change. How many times have I told you that your pants have to cover your *entire* backside?"
3. "Noah, when is the last time you brushed your teeth? Just now? Really? Then come over here and let me—yep. Didn't think so. To the sink!"

Here I am, on the cusp of coming back to the use of what I once knew. With all three children now in school and more self-sufficient than ever, I'm having to wake my brain from its coma as I contemplate doing something in addition to mothering. Toes over the precipice, I am looking down and holding my breath and exercising some kind of great big faith.

Because what if I've forgotten it all?

The evening news is now a rare treat for me. I know few greater pleasures than sitting on the couch with the dishes soaking in the sink to get a thirty-minute crash course in current events. Matt loves to start the morning with talking head political roundtables. I'll shuffle not-totally-awake into the kitchen, and he'll say, in passing, things like, "Can you believe that plane crash in France?" And then I'll moan,

"Wait, *what plane crash in France*!?" because another huge thing has happened in the world and I'm the last one to know. Like I'm not cool enough to be included on the world's text thread, busy as I am extricating myself from dust bunnies and dirty hands.

Last year, I talked to my friend Emily. She has a master's in counseling. She also has small children. She taught occasional yoga classes during their preschool years as a way to generate a little extra income, but motherhood was her full-time job. Then, when both her kids were in school, she began to explore the possibility of going back to work. In not much time, she landed a job in human resources at T. Rowe Price. She was thrilled—and also terrified.

"What if I don't know what I'm doing?" she asked me.

"You will! They wouldn't have hired you if they didn't think you were capable of doing the job." I could tell her this confidently because I knew it was true for her. I could see it from my vantage point, outside of her life looking in. But was it also true for me?

Emily's first few anxious weeks of workforce reentry gave way to courage and certainty. She remembered how to "do" things, things that didn't involve a pack of baby wipes or a sippy cup. What she'd temporarily sacrificed hadn't been lost after all.

It had merely been on hold for a while.

•   •   •   •   •

While my husband was working for the State of Maryland, we had opportunities to do some amazing things, not the least of which was traveling overseas with diplomatic convoys. I was a stay-at-home tagalong mom. This was a benefit to not working—we had chances to travel that didn't require me to take time off. Which wouldn't have mattered anyway, I guess, considering that when you're a mother, you're pretty much always on the clock. Packing for our trip to Ireland was an agonizing affair. I was high strung and shrill as I told Matt I had nothing to wear. And how were we going to get all Noah's baby stuff on the plane? Not helping matters was the fact that I was still wearing maternity clothes with an eleven-month-old at my side. Our entourage included a number of professionals with impressive résumés. I wasn't sure what to wear and was still about twenty-five pounds overweight. I felt like a big, incoherent blob. Like a breast-feeding Jabba the Hutt.

I have a few pictures from that trip. St. Patrick's Cathedral, Trinity College, the Guinness factory, but I'm barely smiling. That's because I had practiced my photo face in the mirror and realized the broader my smile, the more evident my dimples. And the more evident my dimples, the deeper they indented the fat in my face, squeezing my cheeks up into my eye sockets and making me look like a yam. The semi-smile made it look like somewhere in my face there were bones actually holding my skin up.

Then we met Bertie Ahern. At the time, he was the prime minister of Ireland (formally called the "Taoiseach," but I dare you to pronounce it). Mr. Ahern was the head of government. The *whole* government.

The Irish love their babies and they revere their mothers. Everyone from airline stewards to bus drivers took to Noah immediately and asked me questions about the two of us like they'd never seen a toddler. One of the flight attendants on Aer Lingus even held Noah as he cried during the last hour of our very long flight. I was delightfully secure about my lifestyle choice as a SAHM among the "regular" people of Ireland. Until I met Bertie Ahern.

We attended a crowded reception one night in a well-secured tent next to an exclusive hotel. Matt and I stood on the periphery and waited for Bertie to approach. Matt didn't have any sort of direct business request for Bertie. There wasn't anything he wanted. Matt just wanted to meet him. Matt wants what he wants.

Bertie (if you're reading this, I'm guessing our encounter makes us familiar enough with one another to use first names) was maneuvered through the crowd by a tight circle of men in dark suits. People pressed in so densely that Bertie's grey hair was barely visible in the melee. Once he approached, Matt had to "vet" himself briefly with Bertie's security and explain his work with the State of Maryland that had brought him to Ireland to establish further relations, blah, blah, blah. I was mostly trying to quickly swallow the piece of cheese I'd chosen to stuff in my mouth at an unfortunate moment. Then we got fifteen seconds with "the man."

Matt introduced himself and made the requisite small talk. Then he introduced me. Bertie extended his hand.

"What do you do?"

"Well, right now . . . I stay home with my son."

To my great dismay and elation, the prime minister of Ireland responded, "That's wonderful. There's no greater job. Good for you."

I grinned my yam face ear to ear.

Then a member of his security detail whispered something in Bertie's ear. It was probably something like, "You need to start preparing for the Moriarty Tribunal's claims before tomorrow." It could also have been, "These people are nobodies. Let's go." Which is when he was whisked away.

But not before I could awkwardly blurt at his departing back, *"But I'm also a lawyer!"*

• • • • •

There's a commonality of sacrifice to motherhood, a this-for-that substitution that looks one-dimensional. As though there is a simple giving up and a simple getting, a switching of gears and a tidy pressing on. But we mothers know better. We know these phases of our lives intersect with complexity. I love spending time with other mothers who feel the same about the use of their prepartum brains in their postpartum environments. Together we mourn the temporary loss of our wits. And then we are all amazed when what we've done and learned is called into use for the benefit of those we love. Those women who were initially called to a particular line of work somehow always reengage it. I have a nurse friend whose husband was diagnosed with cancer. She's proved a better advocate for his health than I'm sure she ever imagined. My teacher friends instruct their kids in academics with all the professional training they've used to benefit other mothers' children. You know whose teeth are perfectly straight and white? Those of my dentist girlfriend. Another girlfriend with a business degree runs her house like a small enterprise with everything operating on schedule and under budget. How beautifully, how unexpectedly God provides uses for what he gives us.

This mother? Yes, I get the use of what I studied once too. I have used my law degree to write contracts on the side. Sometimes my husband has used my education like a

181

party trick to threaten how cheap it would be for him to sue someone. He does this while I think, *There's no way I will be associated with that.* Then, to ease my doubting heart, the Lord gives me daily stories in my children and opportunities to write them. Which, when you are a mother with a journalism degree, is a perfect fit.

It's a struggle not to compare myself to people in positions that don't require them to be home with small children. Men, childless women, women beyond the age of "Mommy, I need you!" begging. They have a thing I don't: the freedom to read Umberto Eco. If someone had given me one of Eco's books at any time during these years with young children and asked me to identify his use of semiotics in the piece, I'd probably have thrown the book at him. Literally. There's no brain space for symbolism in Italian literature while wearing the same outfit for the third straight day.

And yet.

Because I think God is a laugher, I read this verse the same day of my Facebook brain-shame: "One thing I do: Forgetting what is behind and straining toward what is ahead, I press on toward the goal to win the prize for which God has called me heavenward in Christ Jesus" (Phil. 3:13–14). Forgetting what is behind. For a time. Pressing on toward the goal. I have one chance with my children. They are a prize both present and future. God is doing something new in this part of my story. He is making a way. Impressive party talk, philosophy, simple recall, even: these things wait for me. In this transition to being a mother alone, I struggled with not believing God could restore what I had lost (my brain) because of what I had gained (my children). I didn't believe him good enough to let me have them both. Which was kind of rude and also faithless, but which I will attribute to the mommy brain that's the chief focus of this complaint in the first place. I know the Lord's goodness surpasses my faithlessness. I know he desires to give us good things. I'm pretty sure he also knows my children have substituted my grey matter for the soup of estrogen, cartoons, and fish-shaped crackers.

I have friends who are academics and authors. Their works are well published. I peruse their social media posts longingly but then halt my quiet pining after things that I have put on pause. The Lord is trustworthy. He is building in me something enduring through the small people who depend on me for things beyond my ability to recall that Donna Tartt won the Pulitzer for *The Goldfinch*.

* * * * *

No one tells you that when you get pregnant you're not actually eating for two and that the baby will take what it needs from you without two whole burritos, a basket of chips and salsa, and fried ice cream from Don Pablo's as a regular meal. No, all this bingeing was based on a faulty, old-timey saying about the necessity to double-eat that *no one told me* was a total lie. I must have at some point believed I was going to have a fifty-two pound baby, because nothing stopped me from downing quarts of Ben & Jerry's like it was the last food on earth. Spoon to mouth every night while I poked my belly and called, "Womb service!"

This was my first physical adjustment to motherhood. I had no one to blame but myself. The rest of it, though, I will happily blame on my children. "I lost my ability to sneeze without tinkling because of you!" has gotten plenty of airtime.

As though I had anything to do with it, I applauded myself for my lack of stretch marks during pregnancy. And then I didn't. Because after Noah made his entrance and I could actually rotate at the waist, I found them in silvery waves on both my hips. This was where the tensile strength of my skin had been stretched to its absolute limits. I can't help thinking that it was the result of all that ice cream, because the baby grows in front, in your belly. Not on your hips, which just grow fat. Stretch marks on your hips? That's just plain lack of self-control.

Getting clothing catalogues from which I once ordered is now its own special flavor of ignominy. For example, while Victoria's Secret has apparently decided it's going to rebrand itself as a provider of unmentionables to college-aged models with promiscuity issues, they would do better to include more flannel and oversized T-shirts. These things are necessary, Vicki. They are, in fact, essential. Because if you want the mothers who receive your catalogues to compare themselves to the airbrushed eighteen-year-olds and think about how they really need to get to the gym so they can buy your things, they need to do it comfortably. You know, to build up their resolve. Although as I type this, I realize that perhaps Victoria's Secret hasn't really lost touch with their consumers but rather at age forty-two I am no longer actually their target consumer.

Unless you are a professional bodybuilder, I cannot think of another job that alters one's physical state the way motherhood does. You even smell different. I mean this in both senses: I wear more deodorant than my husband does, and I also have the ability to smell flowers from fifty yards. Which I can attribute to hormones until a brain tumor proves me wrong. The skin on my lower belly wrinkles nicely. Strangely, it's possible to grab a handful of skin above my navel that's perfectly smooth. But move down by a few inches and it's like grabbing a linen shirt that's been caught in the dryer. Oh, and the hemorrhoids. They sometimes like to stick around after you give birth. So that's fun.

Now, a word to other mothers: please, for the love of all things holy, spare us your social media pictures of a perfectly flat stomach six weeks after giving birth. We know that Gwyneth Paltrow got her post-Moses figure through an unattainable regime of psychotic Pilates, vegan eating, professional training, and bird-level dieting, but please. Do any of us have time to make tempe manis or chicken kyerito for dinner? Do you even know what "mirin" and "sucanat" are? Do you know where to find them? Because you're going to need them for the kyerito. You're also going to need a personal chef, because some of Gwyneth's recipes on her lifestyle blog are described as "incredibly complex." Sweet hash, Gwyneth. I have three kids under eleven and various sports practices four nights a week. On off nights, it's church youth group, or riding lessons for Grace, or I am actually "just" trying to write and do not have a full-time nanny like you do. If I sauté some beef cubes for dinner and toss them on paper plates with brown rice, I throw myself a parade.

Let's stick together in this mothering business, shall we? We are very happy for you about your postpartum weight loss, even if our inner voices are saying not so nice things, things that stem from jealousy, even though we know jealousy is a sin. We are trying to be Christlike and celebrate it with you, but it is very hard when some of us can't get our bodies off the couch to exercise—exercise we would do if we weren't exhausted, or busy, or stressed, or had a bunch of children. When I was working at the advertising agency, I strolled across the street to Gold's Gym and worked out five times a week. F-I-V-E. My collection of bathing suits was voluminous, and for good reason. I still have some of these bathing suits. I keep them around to remind myself of what I had once: plenty of free time and a triathlete's metabolism.

However, some of my post-baby-body awesomeness is just due to genetics. The adage about being able to look at your mother and anticipate what you'll look like in the future is mostly true. My mother and I are often told how much we resemble each other. That also means I know what parts of my body are going to fail first. (Kidding, Mom! You're perfect!)

Maybe because of the weight carried by my body during its seven-year tenure as a baby host, food source, and transporter, or maybe because I feel like I do nothing but run after children all day, I seem to be aging faster than I anticipated I would. Like my kids are somehow shifting this process into hyperdrive. You know how the president always leaves the White House with hair whiter than it was when he entered? It's like that. But I don't have any peace treaties or economic stimulus packages to show for it. If anything, I'll leave this stage of life with a bunch of broke people fighting. But hopefully not.

I bent over and heard something today. A crunch. Small, barely perceptible, but there, somewhere below me. Something like stepping on a cracker, a shattering. I kept on through my daily things like watering plants, running dishes, and gathering laundry. When I knelt down to pick up an errant sock I heard it again.

Holy matzo balls. My knees. My forty-two-year-old-not-old-enough-to-be-arthritic knees.

I have been thinking about age lately. I'm not old enough to be getting old, and I'm greatly displeased with the whole process. Especially after discovering that my knees and my wrists have begun to grind like old gears. I thought about it as I looked in the mirror while doing my makeup this morning and reached for a wrinkle cream because, nearly overnight, my face has started to look like an old shoe. I don't mind telling you any of this, because it is real and earnest and, quite frankly, inevitable. For all of us. Though I may be one of the few women foolish enough to pull back the curtain and expose my sagging infrastructure. Beauty is fleeting (see Prov. 31:30). And I don't have the money for Botox. And also, *face poison*. I'm too scared to try anything else "rejuvenating," so I make do with the occasional spackle job. Which, when I've failed to do well, my daughter is super adept at letting me know, because she draws every picture of me with forehead wrinkles. I am getting older and I hate it. Maybe the past few years took a toll on me physically. I feel aged by loss and hardship and the simple accumulation of time, with its path cut through my face and body. I think I see a waddle coming on. I'm not kidding.

But then, after exfoliating and moisturizing and making-up, I pulled a large peace lily into the sink today. It is the biggest of our plants. It doesn't often bloom anymore, but it is over a decade old. I have nursed it and plucked at it over the years. I've repotted it and shuffled it around. Its longevity is something I'm proud of because it was given to us when Matt's father passed. I have somehow, despite my black thumb, managed to keep it alive.

It is as old as Noah, minus three months. It has lasted exactly that long. I cannot look at it without thinking of its age, and also what it represents and how long it has blessed our home.

It is my "Noah" plant, the one by which I gauge his years, and remember how he laid on his daddy's chest in Grandma's house in pale blue fleece jammies the weekend of the funeral. It is also my "Matt" plant, because I remember how the kindness of its offering by our church pleased my husband after his father's passing. It is my "Grace and Jesse" plant because they love its size among the other plants and have been known to hide things in it. And it's my plant, reminding me of all the things I've been and seen in those eleven years. It reminds me of who I am now.

This plant is old, as far as plants go. It has embellished three homes, seen three children, sat in a host of pots. It has taken in sunlight of varying degrees. It has decorated both hospitable and inhospitable places. It's likely no one but me looks at our plant and sees what I do. To my family, it may be simply green and slightly faded at the edges. Its stalks aren't nearly as straight as they once were, and the last time it actually grew a flower was in 2009. But I feel a kinship with this plant. I have kept it alive. I have been kept alive myself. And not by my own power. I have been pruned and watered, replanted and snipped by a greater Master Gardener. I've occupied different spaces, had different roles. I am, like our lily, fading a bit. I don't bloom the same as I once did. We are, both of us, acquiring years.

But I can look at this plant and see my husband and my children. I see the path we've traveled and how we've grown as separate people and as a family together. The plant and my aging self have lived. The things on us that fade prove we have been alive. Now I don't mind the old plant—my lines or my fermenting brain—so very much.

thirteen

Other People('s Children)

No one tells you that after you have a baby, you're going to stand on the edge of a chasm between "used to be" and "what is" and think to yourself, *Can I do this? Are we going to be ok?* Because really, what makes you think you're capable of running things? New mothers know by heart, without being told, that things will change. What we don't know is just how much.

We worry right from the start of the whole process of people-making. We worry about getting pregnant, we worry through the pregnancy, and we worry about whether we'll have to leave our babies for work once they're born. We worry about ever again being able to serve a purpose other than "mother." We worry that our children will not be healthy or kind or fulfilled in life. We worry about all of it. I think our extra X chromosome just permanently hardwires stress to the "on" position.

At some point, parenting may even become solemn, nearly joyless. The worry can sap the good stuff right out of it.

I had these expensive degrees, the evidence of which were dusty certificates hanging in the back of the house somewhere. I had cashed out my investments, bid adieu to my co-workers, and taken the leap. But not before I felt the need to elevate parenting to a liturgical level of commitment. I was ready to strip all the bliss from motherhood and really buckle down. I was going to be the most active, supremely dedicated mother I knew. I was glad I'd left work for my children. I felt no regret, which in turn made me feel guilty. And guilt about not wanting to return to work, about actually *wanting* to be home all day with kids, with no "real" employment? It encouraged me to work all the harder at a job with few concrete, obvious boundaries.

As a SAHM, you don't have to answer to a boss in the morning after you get to work, for example. This part is nice. But you will have to push a child out of your face in the morning before your eyes are even open, and figure out breakfast before your toddler starts chasing the dog with a knife.

For some of us, the unstructured nature of parenting and its absence of hard parameters is refreshing. It allows us to focus on the essential components of the task at hand—of just being with our kids—without being caught up in the machinery of a workplace. For me? It was more like, "Wait—you mean no one expects me to start at a certain time? There are no rules here? Can't someone just give me a project? *What am I supposed to do with all this time and these kids?*"

These open days of mine were obtuse. So I built a daily structure that gave me the comfort of the work world, because it was all I'd known. Otherwise it was just a house and three kids and me, just me, only me, doing this daily thing with these kids who were looking to me for the next move. I was the boss. And I'd never been a boss. So I did the only thing I knew how to do. I installed the architecture of a workday to comfort my restless soul.

Breakfast at 7:30, laundry at 9:00 while baby plays, lunch at 11:00, nap time at 12:00, playtime with the older kids, an hour of cleaning at 1:30, baby up at 2:30, afternoon activity at 3:00 (pray for Daddy to be home early), plan dinner at 4:30 (cry because a grocery store trip with three children is required), dinner at 6:30, and hand kids off to Matt (so I could hide in the closet and surf Facebook). In the course of this day, I interspersed glowing bouts of praise, plenty of treats, a maniacal check for any hidden household hazards, compulsive hand sanitizing, and repetition. And repetition. And repetition.

Guess what? I was tired all the time. My days didn't develop organically, they churned like gearwheels. "Quality time" was actually "all the time," and "all the time" times three is impossible for a normal human. Even one with an adamantium skeleton.

So listen, the extensive parameters we sometimes put on mothering might be more a function of what *we* need rather than what *our children* need. Without really knowing what to call it, I realized I was kind of "over-parenting." And the older they got, the more I over-parented. I remembered recently my own childhood in the 1970s and the way the four of us kids were in the world, really in it, with dirty fingernails and a busted arm or two and a sense that we could stand on our own two feet because we'd been given the chance to try.

I am a product of that era, the one that seems nearly magical to me now, the one in which kids were thrown outdoors to play with a pledge that they had to come back for dinner and not a moment earlier. That era when housewives were fine "just" being housewives, and parents were the law, and kids came home with scraped knees, and we were taught to fold laundry or do the dishes or mow the lawn as soon as our parents figured we didn't risk losing a limb. Facebook, iPhones, and Twitter had yet to be invented, so there didn't exist the dilemma of sharing, sharing, sharing. People talked instead of texting, and they actually looked each other in the eye when they did. Dinner was a family affair, and you never once contemplated telling your parents that you didn't like what was being served. When you were bored, you made your own fun without a grown-up having to jump in and eliminate your tedium of life. You were dropped off at basketball practice and picked up when it was finished, without a grown-up in the stands waving a "congrats for showing up!" flag. There were no trophies for participation, and school was your job, and you knew the rules, which were ironclad. You weren't dragged to chess, and archery, and lacrosse, and swimming all in the same season to determine if you were "gifted" and in order to fill every unscheduled hour of your young life. Also, who had the money to dump into the suckhole of passing adolescent fancies? If you started something you saw it through to the end, with no excuses in between. You were self-sufficient enough to let yourself into the house until your parents got home and, for the most part, you could be trusted not to burn it to the ground.

Parents can do too much. You, friend, are a finite resource and these ankle biters need a couple of limits. I remember my mother's struggles with trying to be the best mother she could be. All of us want goodness for our children—we are motivated by their future success and happiness. But my mom's whole heart was in this job of mothering. So much so that, as she chased the four of us around the house in a game of tag on a summer day, she fell into a rabbit hole and broke her ankle. So I guess we weren't really ankle biters as much as ankle breakers. Breaking something is 110 percent commitment. I've never broken something in the pursuit of parenting. So clearly, Mom, you win.

But my parents took much-needed breathers too. They had regular weekends together, away, just the two of them. And they installed limits. Though they loved us, though they were wholly committed, though we were their highest calling, they did not hesitate to lay the smack down. We knew what the parameters were at all times. Because only one of you can be the grown-up, and it can't be the one with the lisp who's missing his two front teeth.

My parents allowed my siblings and me to experience the consequences of our actions. That meant soap in the mouth; it meant time-out. It meant discipline. Scripture informed their parenting decisions. On that note, I've found that the more Scripture you know, the more persuasive your parenting. Not only because it contains all the true things but because it is really hard for a six-year-old to argue with: "Children, obey your parents in the Lord, for this is right. 'Honor your father and mother'—which is the first commandment with a promise—'so that it may go well with you and that you may enjoy long life on the earth'" (Eph.

6:1–3). Not that I would condition Jesse's life on his obedience. But maybe.

The Bible addresses discipline extensively, and the Lord himself addresses us as his children. God's dealing with us as both his bride (the church) and his children sets the whole of his instruction upon family imagery. Matt and the children are not just my family. They are an extension of my relationship with God. Which is why, every day, in the small and large moments, I often think, *So this is how God feels . . .* and by this, I mean crazy in love and possibly exasperated at the same time.

But what a perfect paradigm for us! God doesn't leave us guessing. He's so wonderful like that. He says,

> It is for discipline that you have to endure. God is treating you as sons. For what son is there whom his father does not discipline? If you are left without discipline, in which all have participated, then you are illegitimate children and not sons. Besides this, we have had earthly fathers who disciplined us and we respected them. Shall we not much more be subject to the Father of spirits and live? For they disciplined us for a short time as it seemed best to them, but he disciplines us for our good, that we may share his holiness. For the moment all discipline seems painful rather than pleasant, but later it yields the peaceful fruit of righteousness to those who have been trained by it. (Heb. 12:7–11 ESV)

Discipline is for our good, for our children's good. They crave it, whether they realize it or not. It proves we are trustworthy enough to be in charge. Let me tell you that when I see a child running wild through a restaurant without parental intervention, the hair on the back of my neck goes up. Please, do not respond to your poorly mannered child with, "I'm sure you are feeling angry or frustrated right now, but you should really think about coming and sitting down because I think it would be best for you." You snatch said child up, tell them they have lost the opportunity for dessert, and if they do it again they will not be able to have that sleepover with the friend they have been waiting all week to see.

Action, reaction. Choice, consequence. A delightful bonus is that discipline will give you, the parent, rest. *Actual rest.* The Bible tells us that outright. "Discipline your son, and he will give you rest; he will give delight to your heart" (Prov. 29:17 ESV).

My parents did not offer many material rewards, either.

I don't know of a quicker way to turn your child into a spoiled brat than by giving him everything he asks for. And listen, I am very guilty of giving in just to quiet my kids (see previous discussion on bribes). But this always, without fail, comes back to haunt me. It feels just about as regrettable as an impulse buy on a credit card (which I'm still paying off, by the way, though the bunion on my right foot means I can't even wear them but they sure do look pretty in their box). One cannot be the last word in parenting when someone thirty-six inches high is screaming for an action figure they know they'll get if only they're persistent enough. "Can I get a toy?" Jesse asks, with the compulsion of someone who's helming a criminal enterprise. "Can I get a treat?" And I will look down at his little Howdy Doody face while he's petting my hand because he knows I love that—and again, criminal enterprise—and I cave. Which means every time I walk into a store I get asked the same question: "Can I get a treat?"

I have no one to blame but myself. I created this monster.

197

I don't remember this happening in my own childhood. My parents either had better sense than I do or we weren't nearly as convincing con artists. These kinds of limits protect your finances and your sanity. They make for more appreciative children. They make for more spectacular holidays. They make for better manners, because when you finally do give them that treat, the thank-you is automatic. Though think hard before buying toys with bulk pieces, like LEGOs or Lincoln Logs. They're easy to wrap because they always come in rectangular packages, but you will find them around your house for a minimum of a year after they are opened. You are also guaranteed to step on a LEGO brick at some point during the night, and it will press into the soft flesh of the sole of your foot like the devil's pitchfork, causing you to trip or maybe blurt out a not-nice word, so at some point when the kids aren't looking you will just start throwing the pieces away. Maybe.

It's up to you to prove to your children that the things they want are only temporary anyway. All the toys they desire, all the gifts and treats are wonderful and shiny—until they aren't. Because eventually the moths and rust get to all of it. The stuff we get in heaven is what really matters (see Matt. 6:19–21). That's what we're saving up for. As an aside, I encourage liberal use of such theology when, for example, your daughter asks you for yet another pair of boots because while she has the knee-high boots and the sparkly ankle boots, what she really wants is the knee-high sparkly boots, even though she will get four uses out of them before they are outgrown and you're sure she will look like Barbarella, which, no. While you cannot wear "treasures in heaven" on your feet, you can point out to your daughter that she won't die simply from wearing what she has for another season. I sure haven't. (Though I've tried to make excuses to Matt that I will, 70 percent off still not sufficing as a good enough reason. Because my husband doesn't like deals and obviously wants me barefoot.)

Our parents expected our obedience and our participation. There were chores. There was homework. To be fair, the homework was easier, and 2 plus 2 didn't equal fish (thank you, Common Core), but we had to muddle through and figure it out on our own. We got help when needed, but the projects were ours, the assignments were ours, and we took responsibility for all of it. We also realized the privilege of living in a home and having nice things, all of which needed to be cared for, so we participated in the caretaking with chores such as vacuuming, and laundry, and caring for the pets. Despite every affirmation that he would care for his guinea pig, Noah totally preferred playing with it to peeling out the urine-soaked bedding and hosing the cage down. Like that was a big surprise. He is therefore not allowed any more pets of his own. But we also have two barn cats and three dogs. Each child participates in the feeding, watering, and letting out of these animals. Grace has a hermit crab, which I have left solely to her ministrations. I do this because while crabs are crustaceans, and spiders are arachnids, they all belong to the same arthropod family, and I think *arthropod* is Latin for "devil with multiple legs." She does all the crab caretaking things every night. She mists the aquarium and provides fresh water. She feeds freeze-dried mealworms and other things I won't touch. It's amazing how long a $6 animal will last if you completely turn it over to the person who wanted it in the first place. The pet store owner told us that if properly cared for, hermit crabs could grow to the size of a coconut. I think he meant to add, "at an aquarium," because our crab is the size of a dime. I think it's actually shrunk since we brought it home.

Sure, I wake up and sometimes think, *I cannot adult today.* But I'm the boss. I took this job and the stakes are high. And if the five of us are really a unit, someone has to set the rules and encourage cohesion. After all, the troop is only as strong as the members believe they are.

● ● ● ● ●

My kids are bold. They are courageous. And they are confident to the point of maybe needing to rein it in a little bit.

> Mom: "Grace, you've come such a long way in your riding. I'm so proud of you for sticking with it and for getting back on your pony when you fall off."

> Grace: "Yeah. I know. And look how pretty my hair is!"

They stand on their own. They stick up for each other. They are not afraid to explore, and they are willing to try things even if it means they fail. They know our lives don't revolve around them, because they cannot. To do so would be to do our children a disservice. It would be to set them loose into a world where they cannot be the center of attention and to downplay their need for independence and individuality. They must be separate from me. Much as I hate it and want them with me like buds on a tree, and though I want their blooming to be my blooming, they are their own people. As am I. Our identity is first to Christ, and then ourselves, individuals who are strong and capable in our own right.

On one summer Saturday, our family of five set out for the state fairgrounds, where Noah was playing in a lacrosse tournament. As we walked the midway, one attraction soared high above the rest: it was a twenty-five-foot palm tree. It was like a climbing wall you might find in a gym, but instead of a big surface with tons of grab space, the tree was about three feet in circumference. Only one person was allowed to climb at a time. I'd never seen anything like it, and there was probably a good reason for that (read: lawsuit). Jesse had spied it first from the parking lot, and pulled on my hand as we approached.

"Mom! I want to climb dat tree!"

Not a chance, kid, I thought. But instead, I said, "Jesse, that might be too high for you. I don't think that's such a good idea." I thought he'd drop it. How foolish of me. He was relentless. He is Matt's child, after all.

We walked the fairgrounds, and Jesse asked again. First Matt, then me. Again and again. Matt held his hands open and looked at me in a way that meant, *What could it hurt?* Matt is to safety what I am to tennis: meaning he knows it's there but he never follows it. Jesse's face was open and pleading, and he had that bared-teeth smile—more clench than grin—and he held my hands in his and tugged them in a silent gesture of wanting. I made my way over to the line of people waiting their turn to climb. I pulled one of the college-aged operators aside.

"Listen, my six-year-old son wants to try this, but we are going to stand right here, and if I want you to bring him down, you need to do it."

The kid nodded and reached for his Oakleys.

"No, I mean it. Like, you need to do it *immediately.*"

I watched him strap my boy in and perform a safety check, making a mental note of all the connection points, and asking him if he was sure everything was tight enough. I saw the kid's back stiffen. Too bad, bro.

Then Jesse kicked off his shoes, grabbed the base of the tree, and started to climb.

The first ten feet weren't so bad. We cheered him on as he went. People started to gather, looking up at a kid whose comparative size seemed to actually give him an advantage. He was a spider monkey, small and nimble, clearly comfortable with climbing because we have staircases and trees and it's not as if the boy hasn't had practice.

But when he was about fifteen feet above us, Jesse stopped his skyward trekking.

"I'm scared!" he half-moaned, half-yelled.

"You can do it!" I hollered up at him. "You can stop at any time, and you can come back down now if you want. I'm right here. But I know you can do it, Jesse!" I cast a whimpering look at Matt, who answered the question before I'd even asked it.

"No. He's going to be just fine."

Jesse had wanted this, after all. He'd had his heart set on this high-rise challenge. He loved to climb. He wanted to make his brother proud. And after a temporary pause, the rush and the height and the love of a challenge propelled him, and he climbed its whole length. Not just once, but four times. Which at $5 a pop meant I was $20 into a social experiment on bravery, but it was totally worth it.

I took tons of pictures and showed them to Jesse.

"Wow!" he chirped. "Dat is weawwy high!"

And it was. And Jesse climbed it because he had the confidence to try and fail. Because on those occasions that he has? We have been waiting for him with loving embraces and promises that there's always a next time. The way our heavenly Father does with us.

I started out as a helicopter parent. I hovered, I watched, I monitored. I think we all start out a little bit this way. I think we tend to over-parent because we are all a bit convinced that parenting as an endeavor is beyond our ken, and we really need to kill ourselves in order to do it the right way. We plague ourselves with the notion that our children are going to be kidnapped or not get into Harvard. So we work harder at parenting because there's just so much we think can go wrong.

My most highly prized baby gift was a video monitor, which is basically a neurotic mother's closed-circuit security camera. On the small TV played grainy footage of my sleeping baby, and with every shuffle and sigh, I flew into the nursery. Then of course, the baby woke up and I had to restart the whole bedtime routine because my anxiety had gotten the better of me and I was convinced that my child was going to be eaten by his pajamas. Here's the thing about video monitors: if the baby is crying, you're going to know it. You don't need a TV to tell you. Yet I held tightly to my apprehension because it was a security blanket in a new place. It was my concrete thing in a job with no rules, no boundaries, and very little affirmation. If I couldn't control the outcome, I would certainly control the input.

The kids' hotdog pieces were minuscule; grapes were avoided altogether. The playground was scoped for potential evils before play. I came to my first visit with the pediatrician armed with questions so foolish he outright laughed at me. Right to my face. But being tired makes it easier to let go.

Maybe that's why God permits it. If you use up all your energy being anxious about being a mom, you have nothing left with which to actually be a mom. So I exhaled a little. I trusted a little. I patched up hurt things and consoled my children after their losses, and I turned all my own fear over to the Lord. I took Isaiah 50:10 to heart: "Who among you fears the LORD and obeys the word of his servant? Let the one who walks in the dark, who has no light, trust in the name of the LORD and rely on their God." I was in the dark. I was careening through a new "career" with a patchwork approach to doing things right when all I really needed to do was rely more on God. I would be the boss, I would set limits, I would act with confidence, and then I would let my children go.

By the third kid, I'd come rolling in to the appointment with the pediatrician two months after it was due, usually late and usually towing two other children and usually looking at my watch to make sure we weren't late for something else. Second and third kids are also good for helping mothers lighten up. If you have trust issues, I highly suggest having more than one child, the theory being that you have kept one alive so maybe you don't need to sanitize your doorknobs every fifteen seconds. Think of it as a kind of mathematical proof theory with more diapers.

Trusting your children to be in the world and find things out for themselves after so long a period of doing things for them is scary. It's scary like that movie *Arachnophobia*. Do you know what that movie is? A whole bag of nopes. I can't even YouTube it because it makes my stomach hurt. Multiple legs, guys. *Multiple.*

While I did my share of hovering, I can say I was certainly never a tiger parent. Tiger parents should just basically invest in CDs they can cash out later to pay for their kids' therapy. I'm convinced the children of these parents, these violin prodigies with their 4.2 GPAs, are going to either helm major corporations or become serial killers. Dolly Cherukuri is a three-year-old girl who just broke the national Indian archery record. The phrases "three-year-old" and "national record" should not even be in the same sentence unless it's for sleeping, because those parents would totally love it. Dolly's parents have said that when they discovered they were pregnant with her, they "decided to mould her as an archer."[1] Maybe Dolly has awesome and laid-back parents who let her do her own thing, and she just magically picked up a bow and arrow one day at twelve months and her parents were all, "Look at this child! She's gifted!" But I doubt it. I think "tigering" was involved. I cannot tiger. I am too much of a lover of my babies. I'm not willing to take the risk that they will grow up and be miserable like Andre Agassi, who, in his 2009 biography *Open*, made public his hatred of his father, who made him pick up a racket as a toddler—but really, the whole time, he hated tennis.

Also, I cannot tiger because I'm just a little bit lazy.

Because here's the thing about being a mother: it's hard. You know that. We feel how hard it is every day. Even when they can take themselves to the bathroom or make their own snacks. And these were things that I thought were the zenith of parenting: once my children had mastered the basics of continuing to live, I would be home free. The higher-level stuff would be a cakewalk because I was so dang tired I would do anything to just get to the point where I was rested enough to actually worry about when Grace was old enough to wear makeup. I didn't know that I would just be replacing one type of difficulty for another. This is why motherhood is *really* hard: it's because the whole job is designed to help these people become independent of you. And everything in your gut wants them, on some plane, to need you forever. Motherhood is the only profession on the planet whose purpose is completely at odds with your most basic desires, and you have to do the job anyway. The guy at the sewage treatment plant probably hates the smell, but at least he gets paid and that's reason enough to keep him coming back. He just does it, day in and day out, without some future knowledge that it's all leading up to doing something that feels more impossible than it already is.

You? You have to teach your children to walk and feed themselves and dress so that they don't leave the house looking like circus clowns. You have to teach them how to ride a bike, and what manners are, and that they need to hold the pencil this way to draw the letter *w*. And once you're past all that, then you have to teach them how to be in the world—how to act and talk, how to treat people, how to love mercy and walk humbly (see Micah 6:8). And the whole time you're doing it, you're constructing the scaffolding around them as they grow so that you can take your hands away and they will finally, one day, stand on their own.

No one tells you how much that part is going to hurt.

Geography

The answer to all writing, to any career for that matter, is love.

Ray Bradbury

fourteen
The Continental Divide

Despite the beauty of this journey, with so much gained and so much richness with which I've been blessed, despite all of the good, I sometimes hear a thing in the shadows that I've had to work hard to ignore. When I'm at my most vulnerable, and I'm doubting the valuable work of my every day and wondering if the near things will pay off in all the ways they could with the people who matter most, I try to ignore a lie:

Mothering alone is not enough. Do something more.

I know I'm not alone. I know other moms feel it sometimes too. Maybe it explains the rise in creative activities like "paint nights." These are innocuous gatherings of women that involve some wine and snacking, where an art teacher hands you acrylic paints and a canvas and you are lightly "instructed" on the principles of painting a picture of a flower or a pair of flip-flops. But here is a paint night principle: most attendees are women, and most of these women are moms. They enjoy a night out with their girlfriends, sure. But do you know what happens when they get down to the business of painting? These women suddenly go all ninja with silent dedication. They are hushed and intent with screwed-up faces, and they work like they're angling for a spot at MOMA. There runs between these mothers the unspoken inkling that these paintings will prove they can still make something other than children. "Paint night" might as well be called "prove it night."

I should know. The last time I was at a paint night, we were told to craft a beach scene with a palm tree. On the far ocean horizon, we were to paint a boat. I fastidiously mixed the perfect combination of yellow, white, and brown for the sand. I shaded the palm tree with a steady hand. Then, the boat.

My boat was a six-sail schooner.

I took it home to show Matt.

"Huh. A little bit overboard, don't you think?"

Well, naturally. That was the point.

I'd wanted the schooner to be something more than just a boat. I'd wanted to nail that glorified paint-by-numbers so bad that I'd exhibited a freakish dedication to a social activity that was supposed to be just a good time. Why? Because it wasn't just a painting or a social get-together. The painting was *me*, you see. The painting was proof that a SAHM could still produce something, that there was some kind of ability left in her somewhere. I'm aware of this now. I can say that, looking back, after discerning that lie among all the truths of motherhood.

Yet this lie led me down the path of a half dozen half-baked work-from-home ideas that were the trappings of early motherhood.

·   ·   ·   ·   ·

First was day trading. Day. Trading. Like I was just going to pick it up. Like I would figure it out the way one figures out how to make a peanut butter and jelly sandwich. You know, with no particular financial shrewdness and no history of investing outside of checking the "medium risk" box when selecting mutual funds for my 401(k).

I subscribed to *Investors Business Daily*. I bought Warren Buffet's *How to Make Money in Stocks*. I followed the markets online. I took notes from CNN financial analysts. I scoured the paper and web for relatively undervalued investments that I thought had the potential to take off. I was convinced I was going to find the next Apple. It was mentally and emotionally exhausting. I had the stock ticker constantly running on the TV, and I had to beat the market each day by making it to the computer before the bells sounded. Plus? It appears "medium risk" may have been a mischaracterization. As it turns out, I am actually "no risk." I'm more of a 100 percent money back guarantee type of investor, which doesn't make you diddly squat in day trading. If you're looking for the next McDonald's IPO, you won't find a buy-in at $5 a share.

I'm sure it comes as no surprise that I didn't make a million dollars. There was no explosive transformation by trading in penny stocks. I made a whopping $2,000 over the course of twelve months. This works out to $166.66 a month, or $5.55 per day. And $5 was pretty much the ceiling on what I was willing to pay for a stock. Therefore, I was netting about $0.55 a day. In addition to the $2,000 I made that year, I also made myself a severe case of gastritis chasing down the "next big thing." Day trading is not for anxious people.

Then there was eBay. Oh, how there was eBay.

It is possible to make a very good living on eBay. I find, however, this is the distinct privilege of people who have experience buying and selling things in other places. In stores, for example.

This eBay experiment of mine began simply enough. In the beginning, it was a place to unload unwanted or unused trinkets and outgrown baby items. But once I started getting paid for things I was finding in my house, I about lost my mind with the rush.

"I am a wizard!"

I began scouring closets for clothing and picking through boxes of home decorations. But there was an end. At some point, one runs out of things to sell and must, if one wants to continue in such an endeavor, supply one's growing "business" (i.e., obsession) with actual inventory.

Naturally, I picked the most expensive inventory category I could find.

Why not designer accessories?

Why not? Well, for a lot of reasons: it is hard to source, it is hard to front the cash while you're waiting for a sale, and it is hard to unload because only a certain percentage of the population is willing to pay $750 for a handbag.

None of these reasons occurred to me at the time. What occurred to me was how much fun it was going to be to drive to Washington, DC, and meet with an importer who made regular trips to the outlets in Florence, Italy, and from whom

I could buy Gucci handbags at a 50 percent discount. In this period of motherhood, when I was "all-in" with three kids underfoot, I was scrambling for something extra. I needed that sliver of purported meaning, that thing I could do beyond the same tasks every day without anything to show for it. When day trading petered out, I bought *eBay for Dummies*, believing once again I could read my way to mastery of just about anything. My online store Rue de la Mode was born.

My store stocked scarves, shoes, handbags, and jewelry. I dug online and through sales racks to fill in the collection of bigger ticket items I was buying from my importer at steep discounts and then resold everything to the public at a price below retail value but above what I had paid. All this involved comparing prices online for identical merchandise to price it appropriately. Then I had to build the storefront with SEO tools, and coding, and peacock feathers, and whatever else you have to put into your internet presence so people can find you. Then I bought a light box and painstakingly photographed, from every angle and in every light possible, every piece of merchandise I sold. At my most active, I ran inventory at about fifty items a month. Moving just 20 percent of it meant that I had to print invoices, handle billing, collect payment for, and ship ten items a month. Then I had to research, purchase, photograph, and replace the same quantity in my store. This was after I had created collateral material for marketing—business cards, a store brochure, and a legal statement about the verified authenticity of each item I was selling. There is an epidemic of counterfeit merchandising online, and every Jane Doe who hangs a shingle can claim that her obviously plastic handbag is a Dior and there's only so much eBay can do. All my store policies were airtight, and as a lawyer I felt particularly accountable. Late nights, low lamps, sitting at a small desk in our bedroom while Matt dozed, I found myself engrossed with reseller policies and upcoming sales.

Can you imagine how easy all of this was?

For the same reasons that I abandoned day trading, my one-year experiment with online selling came to an end: specifically, an unhealthy ratio of time to money. I wouldn't necessarily say I have a head for business, though in the end I did come out in the black. I would, however, say I have a head for creativity. Like creative ways to buy stuff so that I could look my husband square in the face and tell him a certain purse was inventory when really I was just waiting the appropriate amount of time to move it into my closet.

After these two moderately successful ventures, I decided maybe I ought to just go back to our family budget and see where we could cut some fat. Because here's the reality: we were really fat.

One morning, I woke to find Matt fuming in the kitchen. He was standing over our Mr. Coffee pot, obviously trying to keep his cranium from detonating all over the kitchen walls.

"The coffee machine is broken!" He was flipping buttons and opening and closing the top.

"Oh, c'mon!" I howled. I'm at a three-cup-a-day minimum. The first cup is drunk quickly, like a bottle of water after a marathon. The second cup is finished before I remember I haven't eaten breakfast. Number three is sometimes reheated in the microwave because it starts to cool and I need it hot, scorched-tongue hot, before I sit down to my computer to work. Now Matt was standing over our broken coffeemaker and I was noting the time to see how long I had before developing a migraine from caffeine withdrawal.

"Well, we'll just go to Walmart and get another one. I don't think they're that expensive. But please, if you don't take me to the 7-Eleven to get coffee on the way, you're going to have to peel me off the roof."

On the way to Walmart, a conversation ensued that went something like this:

Matt: "I want one of those massive Braun stainless steel things with a built-in grinder for beans."

Sarah: "When, if ever, have you ground beans for our coffee?"

Matt: "I haven't, but I'd really like to start."

Sarah: "Really? I have literally never heard you say one thing about this until right now."

Matt: [silence]

Sarah: "I mean, really?"

Matt: "Think about how nice it would be to have fresh-ground coffee in the morning."

Sarah (haltingly, hesitatingly): "Well, ok . . . let's just see how much it costs."

What it cost was $150. It was the size of a television with a manual the size of a textbook. I know this because despite my protestations that the $29 Mr. Coffee was going to work perfectly fine, and we might not really have the time or desire to grind our own coffee in the morning, we ended up with the massive Braun stainless steel coffeemaker.

But only because someone gifted one to us.

A good friend of ours who—ironically enough, and again, God is funny—ran his own financial consulting firm, called us just as we were headed to make the purchase. He had a giant coffeemaker that his family no longer had a use for, and would we be interested in taking it off his hands?

Oh, would we!

"God gave us what we wanted! He answered our prayers!"

The space shuttle java maker was a great addition to our kitchen and our morning routine. For a week. Until we realized we had to buy specialized mesh filters for the thing. That could only be purchased in specific, totally inconvenient places. Which we did. Then it was back to being awesome. Until we discovered it had a leak and woke up to coffee all over the counters and floor one morning.

So we went back to Walmart to buy a Braun coffeemaker of our own. *And* a coffee grinder to go with it. Because when you've had the best, it's hard to take a step back, you know?

The purchase was pretty benign, as purchases go. It was just a coffeemaker. It was "just" $150. But I was at a point in my life where money had taken on a new meaning. Without a regular income, and only moderate success in my money-making efforts, I wanted our purchases to be as close to necessary as possible. When getting three children ready for school in the fall required two shopping carts and a bank loan, spending $150 on a coffeemaker was an unnecessary extravagance.

Another unfortunate discovery: nothing expensive ever stands on its own. Expensive things beget more expensive things.

Want a boat? Storage slip, cleaning and servicing, fuel.

Want a house? Repairs, furnishings, taxes.

Want a massive Braun coffeemaker? Coffee beans, specialty mesh filters, stupid and unnecessary accessories your husband buys at the store because they sound like a "good idea."

So we threw another $100 or so at the coffee machine and our insane caffeinated plan to develop the perfect pour.

Then it broke. Of course it broke. *The second one broke.*

And you know what we did? We went back to Walmart and bought the $29 Mr. Coffee.

The same Mr. Coffee that's been sitting on our counter for five years.

● ● ● ● ●

My current life is so separate from the one I led before this transition that it seems very nearly like one lived by someone else. My co-workers and bosses are things of memory. Stacking books or prepping for a pitch could all be left at any point. I could dabble. Whatever piqued my interest, I followed like a dog on a scent, changing course without children to consider. After babies, I crossed that yawning ravine separating two very different worlds. I've carried things with me into this new land. Some of them are useful here, others I've had to shed like a skin. My love for people, my quickness to apologize, my ability to accept responsibility for screwups large or small have proven beneficial to my children. And on this note, always apologize to your kids. Do it often and quickly. Do it, because the following maxim is true: it is easier to build a child than to repair an adult. It is also cheaper, because some psychologists don't participate with insurance.

My incessant drive and my tendency toward perfectionism were real downers when it came to parenting. Bosses love these traits. But they will turn the people who live with you into a band of shrieking hyenas if you don't shuck them off. Vigilance, however, is a blessing to corporations and kids alike: on the one hand, it prevents lost cases and lost revenue. On the other hand, it prevents a child from flushing toy trains down the toilet behind your back, necessitating a plumber. *Plus* lost revenue.

A way with words has served me well in both stages of my life. I was once paid for my ability to communicate. That same ability proved useful when I stammered my way through the "What do you do for a job, Mommy?" question. The second time. Because the first time, my response carried with it a soupçon of vagueness tinged with a hint of unintentional blame. I rambled something like, "Well, Mommy is a lawyer but she gave that up so she could stay home with you guys and be home all the time and not go to a job. So mostly Mommy cooks and cleans and does laundry and helps you with homework and watches baby Jesse."

Grace: "So, you're like a babysitter? Or a maid? Which?"

Think, Sarah. Give them something good. Go!

Mommy: "Well . . . kind of both . . . I guess."

Later, I had learned to fine-tune my response, remembering that, as is always the case with words, the power of a good edit cannot be overstated. Neither can the power of memory, because children don't forget much, and I didn't want my three to look back on the history of their formative years and remember their mother as a maid. I wanted to communicate the essence of my job responsibilities as simply but meaningfully as possible.

"Mommy was a lawyer, but right now her only job is mommy. She loves you guys so much she wanted to leave her job and be with you all the time. Because she loves you so much. Did I tell you that Mommy loves you? Don't forget, Mommy loves you!"

Optimistically, I opened myself up to questioning, envisioning the speeches my kids would deliver at their wedding rehearsal dinners as they toasted me: me, the mother who had made so many sacrifices, the mother who had worked so hard to build a solid foundation upon which they could brick together their adult selves.

Instead, Grace patted my hand.

"It's ok, Mom. We know you love us. You can go back to work."

* * * * *

A new part of my life on this side is poor health. It's a part to which I've become married and have learned to balance with my children who need more than I sometimes feel capable of giving. I have a weird auto-inflammatory illness that goes by the easy-to-pronounce moniker "Behcet's disease." It took more than three years to diagnose my Behcet's, with a host of people calling me a hypochondriac along the way. I will spare you the details, because I know you're just going to Google it anyway. Don't eat beforehand, though.

When I turn on the TV and Phil Mickelson comes on in a commercial explaining how Enbrel helped cure his psoriatic arthritis, I always smirk. I am getting monthly infusions of something like Enbrel, and it's supposed to kick the Behcet's out of my body. It's not a cure but rather a hope for remission, really. So to hear Phil wax poetic about how you should ask your doctor if Enbrel is right for you, and that the side effects include sudden death, and that you need to stay out of the sun while on Enbrel because you might become a toad always makes me laugh. Either Phil's Enbrel is working really well or he is being paid so much to endorse it he doesn't care if it does. Thus far, my own medication's left me unimpressed.

But I don't mind the infusion days so much. When they started, I was a shaking mess. I was led down a wing of the clinic reserved for the lab and the infusion room. The fact that they kept us out of the way of the main clinic space made me think that what was behind door number two was not going to be a trip to Maui. No, it appeared at first glance like a scene out of *Dying Young*. Looking at six people hooked up to IVs and blood pressure cuffs while nurses scurry in between them can really set off a girl's holy poop-o-meter. But the patients were eating snacks and watching the flat screen TV mounted on the wall. They made small talk, flipped through magazines, joked with the nurses. What's more, my fellow patients were sitting in leather recliners. There is not a chair in my home as comfortable as my infusion chair. Maybe it wasn't going to be so awful.

I underestimated how hard it would be explaining to my children, two of whom struggle with severe anxiety, why I came home with a bandaged arm every six weeks. Once again, some wordsmithing was needed. Noah's face went ashen when I explained the concept of an infusion, and told him that what I was being injected with was technically chemotherapy. Noah knew some sick people got chemotherapy, and not all sick people got better.

In retrospect, this was a poor choice of words. I probably should have taken a step back from all the "We're not going to use euphemisms in this family!" garbage. It wouldn't have killed me to just say it was medicine.

Jesse very simply and without emotion asked if I was going to die, and if so, when.

I think we know which one of them is going to get everything when I do.

I can stand at a distance and realize now that this disease reared its head after I'd made the decision to be home full-time with my children because God knew that I'd be better able to withstand it. I don't need a boss's permission to take a day off for treatment, or the next day when I feel like I've been beaten by a bag of hammers because of two IV bags' worth of an aggressive medication. In some ways, it is emotionally easier too. Once I'd gotten my children to fully believe that no, I wasn't going to be dying anytime soon (sorry, Jesse), I came to enjoy little fingers in mine while we laid on the bed together, and little heads on my shoulders while we watched *Beverly Hills Chihuahua* for the fifty-third time.

Their presence has been a comfort to me when I needed comforting. This is another of parenting's delightful surprises. It's not always the grown-ups who provide the grown-up things.

•   •   •   •   •

Humanity's lot is to work. And I have always worked, but in different ways, as one who's paid and as one who isn't. I have been both employee and mother; I have produced different things on each side of this continental divide. I knew I would love my children. This is a commitment we make in our minds as another person begins to grow under our hearts. The loving is easy.

It's the sacrificing that's hard.

It never seemed feasible to me to give up years and years of schooling and thousands and thousands of dollars to stay at home and learn the "backpack" song from *Dora the Explorer*. My value was so neatly calculated in my previous life I didn't think I'd be able to stomach slinking past my co-workers with my armful of diplomas and a solitary plant on my way to the lobby, where my husband rocked my son's stroller in steady fashion and my soon-to-be-former co-workers opened the shade to peek in and giggle at a tiny, round face. The giving up was going to be hard, the substituting "worker" status for "mother" status. It was. Yes, every second of the sacrifice was hard.

Studs Terkel interviewed a mother on welfare with five children in *Working*. Jesusita Novarro said these words in 1972, but her perspective on childrearing is as compelling now as it was then:

> A job that a woman in a house is doing is a tedious job—especially if you want to do it right. . . . Some men work eight hours a day. There are mothers that work eleven, twelve hours a day. We get up at night, a baby vomits, you have to be calling the doctor, you have to be changing the baby. When do you get a break, really? You don't. This is an all-around job, day and night. Why do they say it's charity? We're working for our money. I am working for this check. It is not charity. We are giving some kind of home to these children. . . . I pray a lot. I pray to God to give me strength. . . . It's his kid. He just borrowed him to me.[1]

Jesusita reminds us that children aren't ours to keep but ours to steward for a time. Mothering offers no break, until the break when our children leave us for their own adulthood. It's hard and it will hurt in the end. So why pursue it at all? Why this longing for children that nags a woman's heart? It makes no sense as valuation goes. It cannot be neatly calculated. It is not predictable. It is unrelenting and repetitive. The daily investments of effort and time and instruction are made strictly with an eye toward a later yield—a yield that if we are lucky will sometimes flash out at us in brief moments, where character and strength and the ability to cut one's own food appear in time. But the rest is always input, with a prayer toward the output that will represent the best of what we've done.

If, as Terkel wrote, the goal of working is to be remembered, to find meaning in the day-to-day of things, he has made a case for motherhood as the highest profession. The legacy we leave in the work of parenting is *people*—people who remember us because of how we've guarded them and cared for them. The meaning of raising people to go on after us pours from every crevice of the smallest motherhood things. The sandwich made teaches care. The fight interrupted teaches meekness. The apology given teaches humility. The face kissed teaches love.

Not a single moment of this job is wasted, not even the simple moments of just showing up.

My mother's choice to simply be present on days she likely doesn't even remember, when the heat outside was too much and she would spread a cool white sheet over our orange shag carpeting and bring us "black cows," a combination of Coca-Cola and vanilla ice cream—this presence, I still cherish. For long stretches we sat together on that sheet, watching *G.I. Joe* and *Jem and the Holograms* cartoons. And

I remember her with us. Not doing anything. Just sitting. Just being present.

I've since learned that the Jem dolls I once had are now collector's items, going for $125 a pop. I've long since parted with mine but wish I'd had the foresight to keep them as a way to remember those summer days, heavy and still and full of one another. For Grace, of course.

Just kidding. For eBay.

●　●　●　●　●

I've traveled from someplace predictable and consistent to a place where not much makes sense. There's no structure over here, and the few boundaries there are my children seemingly exist to cross. I've grown accustomed to hands in my food when something I'm eating looks delicious to a child who literally has the *exact same thing* on his plate. I've become used to picking another person's nose with my finger because there was nothing else to use and I did not want my son going out into the world looking like no one cared about his dirty nose. I know what it is to have my bras worn as hats, to have my soft belly discussed in public, to lose the use of my bed for sleeping and relinquish it instead to epic wrestling matches. Having children means privacy is always elusive, the house is always a mess, and things are never done. I live my life in the superlative, and I adore it.

Madonna said once, "I think I was pretty self-obsessed until I had children." You *think* you were pretty self-obsessed before kids? No, Madonna, you *were* self-obsessed before kids. (Actually, from what I can tell, you still are.)

It seems impossible to be self-obsessed after kids. You lack not only the time for it but also, if you're a halfway decent parent, the interest in being self-obsessed. At some point, you're forced to recognize that it's not all about you anymore. If you're lucky, you reach this conclusion as you're looking down into a hospital bassinet and realizing that maybe changing her diaper comes before your need for a pastrami on rye from the cafeteria downstairs. This conclusion makes everything afterward that much easier. If you persist in a wrongheaded notion that you are the center of the universe, you will just be perpetually ticked off. Because your children will think they are, too. In the same way only one of you can be the boss, only one of you can be the baby. Despite what your husband thinks.

Everything I had changed after I became a mother. I could still get dinners out, or breaks in my day, but it all required a babysitting roster as long as my arm and cash to blow. Disposable income is hard to come by when you have kids, because just going to the movies with them will require a celebrity bankroll. Even going out to eat in a public place with children requires a lengthy explanation on what exactly coleslaw is, that crayons are for coloring pages and not each other, and that surf and turf is not an acceptable dinner choice.

I was valued in both stages in my life, but differently. My value has come in the form of a raise or a paycheck, predictable and steady, quantified by decimals and commas. It has been measured in withholdings and benefits, tallied in bonuses and overtime. But it has also been erratic and random, and smeared with jelly and grass-stained and in need of a shower. It has been loud and demanding and full of knock-knock jokes that I've heard a hundred times. This is the strange beauty of being a woman, isn't it? We possess the capacity for infinite personal evolution. The nature of our relationships and our work will be in constant flux during our lives. Our value can be different from one stage to the next.

But our worth—the essence of who we are underneath what we might offer the world—does not, will not change. This is the guarantee that girds our lives.

No matter the stage, no matter the compensation, our worth is solely who we are in Christ.

Christ, who defines the arbitrary things of the universe as an ordered part of him. Christ, who uses our children and our love for them as a reflection of how passionately he loves us.

Christ, who says we are worthy not because of what we do or even who we raise, but simply because of who we are. *Because* we are.

> Are not two sparrows sold for a penny? Yet not one of them will fall to the ground outside your Father's care. And even the very hairs of your head are all numbered. So don't be afraid; you are worth more than many sparrows. (Matt. 10:29–31)

Here are the "bonuses" Christ gives us: when our six-year-old son looks at us and asks us if he can stay with us forever and ever. Or when he says from between the covers in the early morning, petting our face, "I want to join the army because I want to take care of my country and you." Or when our eight-year-old daughter brings us coffee in the morning because she knows we "aren't a morning person." Or when our eleven-year-old son tells us he loves us and, unprompted, wraps his arms carefully around our waist. Because you were pretty sure he gave up those displays of affection with Thomas the Train.

This is when God, the sparrow-holder, reminds us he is near. Elisabeth Elliott wrote:

> Work is a blessing. God has so arranged the world that work is necessary, and He gives us hands and strength to do it. The enjoyment of leisure would be nothing if we had only leisure. It is the joy of work well done that enables us to enjoy rest, just as it is the experiences of hunger and thirst that make food and drink such pleasures.[2]

Motherhood as work is a most unique profession. It is a type of toil and rest together. It is the angst of hope delayed and the rest of things come to fruition. It is the repetition of our daily care and the peace of knowing our children are cared for. It is the strain of seeking righteousness and the delight of seeing it manifested in our family.

The value of motherhood is children: what they learn, how they grow, that they are.

The value of motherhood is also us: the impact of having changed the world because of those we will leave behind.

My value over here, on this side, is not in what I accomplish. It's in who I accomplish it for. It's found in the faces of the people for whom I've sacrificed so much and from whom I've gotten an even greater measure in return.

Motherhood is the very proof we have lived.

fifteen

The River of Stars

A mother represents all the parts of humanity. She is the chronology of humankind, starting with a tiny tadpole of a person, hidden in a dark and silent place.

The mother is the starting place.

She represents the tiniest parts in life's earliest stages. She is the frightened parts, when she realizes she has left the hospital without a manual on how to raise a baby; the angry parts, when she lacks a moment's peace and the same messes spill all over her once-clean floor; the anxious parts, when the fever spikes or the cries come in the nighttime. She is the beautiful, mysterious parts, when she learns she can love someone just because that person exists.

Philosopher Michel de Montaigne once wrote that "the only good histories are those that have been written by the persons themselves who commanded in the affairs whereof they write."[1] This looks like my personal history. I've had a command of my own affairs, if you can call being haunted by indecision and compulsion a "command" of affairs. But make no mistake. This story belongs to both of us.

You have lain in some hospital bed, somewhere. Or maybe in your own bed near your doula, or in a bathtub with a midwife at your side (I'm impressed, by the way). I wish I could see how happy you were on the day they brought that child of yours to you. There was a feeling like coming off the first dip of a roller coaster when you pulled a tiny set of footie pajamas from a box for the first time. The first time they laid that tiny person on your belly, from where he or she squinted up at you with dark eyes and a red face, I know how you felt. Like a star had exploded somewhere inside of you, dwarfing everything else that had come before it. I feel as though, across time and space, wherever you are, we are connected somehow. We have seen the ugly things and the exhausting things. We have made an uneasy peace with messes and disorder. We have learned the art of bending in places where we once might have broken. We have given up one thing to get another, and we have discovered some things along the way. We have learned that white clothing is the enemy and to run when someone little says, "Uh-oh."

We have learned that this is an all-or-nothing job. Once undertaken, there's no turning back.

Babies are the sweet, small part of this job—the one we think we can do with our eyes closed when we first take it up. We're just tired, we think. Just need a shower and a nap.

Yeah, right.

We eventually get more sleep and more showers, but somehow the work gets harder. It turns out that keeping another person alive is the sort of easy part. Eat, poop, sleep, play.

That's all babies really do. The difficult stuff is broaching the birds and the bees, waiting by the door when curfew's broken, helping heal a broken heart, and explaining that everybody dies.

You will have less puke on your clothes. Maybe you're finally out of yoga pants. But your soul will be weary. There will be days when you think it's too hard, or uninteresting, or unfulfilling. This will matter to no one but you. You can't even take a last-minute vacation without the kind of scramble for childcare that makes the Bay of Pigs look like *Barney*. So you'll have to pick yourself up off the floor where you may have had a good cry because the dishwasher is broken and the boy has drawn all over himself and his sister with permanent marker, and you'll get right back to the children to whom you are connected. Because it's your job.

Everything is related in one way or another, significantly or silently, to the children we've borne. This connects us to our spouses. It connects us to each other.

That's what love does. Love connects things.

Our lives have a current. We are in constant motion, flowing from one stage into another. As our children grow, we move alongside them. We are wives and sisters. We are daughters and friends. But when we are mothers, we are mothers forever. We flow with the strength only God can give us, always forward, despite our own innumerable weaknesses. Even when we yell and cry and feel as if we're standing still. Even when the hardness of doing this job feels like cement around our feet and we think the clock has stopped. Even with all of it, we're still flowing from the place that Eve came, too, where "a river watering the garden flowed from Eden" (Gen. 2:10). Eve, who was wife and worker and mom.

If I were able to prophesy, if I found any talent on this path, let it be my ability to see near things, everyday things, with meaning. Let it be that I recognize my time in sacrifice to my children as a way to carry on my great love for them, that thing which is only a bright reflection of the love Christ has for me.

• • • • •

A few months ago, I found myself at the airport at 5:30 in the morning. There are two things to be said here. First, I hate mornings. Second, I hate airports. But I was enduring two things I hated for one thing I loved: writing. I was headed to a book convention in Orlando to promote *Sand in My Sandwich: And Other Motherhood Messes I'm Learning to Love.* I had enough time to spare that I could get coffee and a bagel. I was already in line when I saw a Starbucks across the aisle. Which peeved me, because I was already committed to what I'd ordered so there was no backing out to get the high-octane stuff I would have much preferred. Also, I was hungry and didn't want to wait in another line. Breakfast at 5:30 a.m. may be too early for the average woman, but for me it's practically lunch because I have the appetite of an all-pro lineman.

At that particular time, on that particular day, at that particular airport coffee shop, the line of customers was all women. One was a college student wearing an oversize tank top with plenty of ennui. Another was an older woman with a quilted cotton handbag and sensible shoes. And right between them was a mother with a baby in a stroller and a toddler in tow. In one brief flickering, I saw the whole of my life all lined up. Each stage. Each milestone.

I was drawn to the young mother who was patching herself together with sippy cups, a falling-out ponytail, and a baby who was having none of this coffee shop nonsense. He was quite nearly at maximum flux capacity, and I smiled at her as I turned around and waved to her babies to make them smile. For a moment, I paused.

In that mostly empty airport, I wanted to pull her aside and say, "I know how this kind of sucks right now. I mean, traveling with little kids is the pits. Like raking leaves in a hurricane, am I right?" And here she would laugh, because I'm hilarious. Then I'd say, "I know you're embarrassed and probably overwhelmed. But don't be. This part is so short. I used to hate it when people said that to me, but it's true. My kids are still elementary school age. They're a little older than yours, and yes, they can do more for themselves than yours can, but I'm still only a few hundred yards down the river from you, and I need to tell you to just be here for a second. In this moment. Be present, because this isn't going to last. You may not feel it, but you're moving, and they are too. The current is pushing all of you forward.

"You won't remember trying to order coffee over the head of your baby who is totally tripping out right now. And he is seriously tripping out. My kids did that too. And always in public places, where they would act like they'd been force-fed Red Bull through a Pixy Stick.

"What you'll remember is sitting him on your lap, with your little girl beside you, watching the sun come up through the airplane window. You'll recall enjoying the little heaviness of him, and your daughter's chubby fingers holding a crayon as she colors on her airplane tray. And you'll thank God that

233

they still give you the paltry bag of pretzels on some flights, because a baby can gum a pretzel all day.

"Wherever you're going with these little stars of yours, the journey is never as long as you think it is. So marvel at their brightness now, while you can. While they are right under your nose. While there is baby fat to squeeze and daily disasters to contend with. Before you send them out in the world to shine on their own.

"They are so amazing. And so are you, tired and amazing mama. Look at the work you've done. At what all that effort has wrought. Look what you've made and built.

"What a vital, lasting job you have."

I didn't say any of this, though. Let's be honest; I was only half awake. I'm lucky if I engage my own children, let alone a stranger, before my first sip of coffee. I still think about her sometimes, though, that mom I was seeing as if through one-way glass. I wish I'd shared some of this with her.

Who knows. Maybe she'll buy this book.

sixteen

Time Travel

Now that I have crossed the divide, I wonder what I would have told myself, as this self of mine prepared for the motherhood journey. What might I have done well to know before I made the transition from worker to mother? There are so many things. Things I wish I'd said to that airport mother, things I wish I could have said to my younger self. Things beyond the standard "You will want this stroller" and "Test the milk on the inside of your wrist" fare. So I am going to take this younger me by the shoulders and force her to sit down and read a letter I wrote to her:

Dear Sarah:
    This is a letter to you, my twenty-seven-year-old self with no children and a flat stomach, the one with the luxury of free time and the use of the whole bed.
    Enjoy these last few months of getting to pee alone. It's going to be fabulous to drop everything and hop

a train to New York City this weekend. I'm kind of jealous of young me, actually. You're not going to be able to drop a lot of things as you get older. You will, however, get to pick up a lot of things. Seriously. There is a hamper in the boys' room. I don't think they know what it's for.

There are some things I would like to share with you that may be of benefit as you enter this new stage of your life. You are something like 15 percent body fat right now, and this will be nothing short of preposterous in a few years. You will gain the equivalent weight of Justin Bieber with your first child, and from that point hence you will be one to three sizes larger than you are now. You will eventually lose (nearly) all the weight, but your hips will be connected to your torso by very loose rubber bands. Don't believe me? Try a squat. See?

Because you joke that travel is your superpower (either anxious about the future or regretting the past, as you are), I am doing you a favor by outlining the things you ought to remember early so that you might save yourself a mess of regret and embarrassment in the face of your life's most acute adjustment and most important work.

So here goes. Twenty things to enrich your life and prevent your head from exploding after you have children:

1. No matter what you're doing, stop it if your child asks you to cuddle. Especially the ones who normally avoid your embrace like the plague. At some point, they will avoid touching you altogether. There will come a point

236

at which your oldest child will tell you, "Stop it, Mom, you're embarrassing me!" just because you are looking at him in public.

2. If there is cake, eat it. Especially on your children's birthdays, because you will regret that you never tasted it when you look back on the family photos, and also because your kid won't understand why you don't get to enjoy that part of his birthday with him. And also, you paid for it, so otherwise it's just wasteful.

3. Walk slower. Breathe deeper. Practice restraint. Your kids will have a hard time keeping up with you when they are little, and they will mostly want to hold your hand. But one day you will find yourself racing to catch up with them. Enjoy the pace while it lasts. You will otherwise regret not savoring things.

4. Take time to listen to your children. It's not multitasking if you're mentally doing other things while their lips are moving. You're just making it harder on yourself when they ask if you have any opinions on how they should handle the fight with Sydney they told you about. Yesterday. When you weren't listening.

5. When they hand you your child in the delivery room, take a moment to smell their perfect head. That sweetness only lasts for so long. After that, it mostly just smells like sweat, or pizza. For some reason, it smells a lot like pizza.

6. Leave your children at least twice a year for a day or more. It may seem impossible the first time, but as long as you find a caretaker who won't actually chain them in the yard, the wonders of modern technology will keep you connected. Cell phones, Skype, iPads, FaceTime: the

technology of your children's generation is expensive but convenient, and this will mean you'll practically be taking them with you. This leaving is important for your marriage and your motherhood. Remember, you are a person separate from them. Your separateness will help them develop separateness of their own. And your husband will have no trouble leaving them whatsoever. Trust me.

7. *When you find yourself at home with children on a snow day, resign yourself to getting nothing accomplished. These days will jack up your perfectly crafted schedule, and a tiny, mutinous army will require twenty-five minutes of preparation for snow play that will last a total of ten minutes. Then they will drag soggy boots and wet mittens all over your house even though you've told them to drop everything at the door. There will be nowhere else to send them after they've exhausted the brief outdoors, so the house that you struggle to keep habitable will descend straight into third-world filth. But you will get to stay in your PJs and eat popcorn with the kids on the couch.*

8. *Unless you are Kate Middleton, you will not look like you did before you had kids. Your hips will have weird proportions (see rubber bands, above), and there's a pretty good chance your stomach will look like an accordion when you bend over. But you can now say your body has truly been used of God. He picked you to introduce another person to the world, after all. This is nothing short of miraculous. There exists no sufficient way to describe the fantastically crazy experience of acting as a human transit system until they pull another*

human out from somewhere below your sternum and put this person on your chest, and you find yourself sobbing because it is terrifying and beautiful at the same time.

9. *That being said, if your kids ask you to go swimming, do it. Don't think twice about the way you look in a swimsuit. In fact, just put on a bikini now, while you're twenty-seven, and don't take it off until you're pregnant with Noah. There will be a point at which you will very much miss the opportunity to publicly appear in a bathing suit without a ton of self-shaming. However, if you want a shortcut, just repeat the mantra, "Looks don't matter." Because they really, truly don't. Don't waste the first few decades of your life trying to figure that out. And remember, your daughter will always be observing the way you talk about your own appearance. You are teaching her what is important, whether or not you use words.*

10. *Be kind to yourself. You will make parenting mistakes. You will blow it. Your children will still love you. If you are kind to yourself, it will help you be kind to your children. It will also help you be kind to others, including other moms. Do not give our gender another chit of cattiness to hold. The pit of meanness in this world is big enough already. You must embody true love, because you have known it yourself.*

11. *Be swift with your apologies. You will be surprised at how far an apology goes with a child. They are quicker to forgive than adults, and they might even follow suit with their own apology when they make a mistake. Not so much with their siblings, but at least with you.*

12. *Your days of jumping on a trampoline are over, friend. You will tell yourself while you're pregnant that Kegels are in your future, and you will be the GI Jane of continence after your kids are born. But it will not happen. At the end of the day, when you find yourself in flannel sleep pants on the couch in front of the TV, even a Kegel—literally, an act with effort so small no one else can see it—is going to seem like too much work.*

13. *All of your children will throw public tantrums at some point. Especially the boys. One of them will also paint with poop the first time you have a new sitter over (this will not be one of the boys). Public humiliation is guaranteed when you're a parent. Do you know what works? To correct the offending behavior and keep on rolling. Sister, you stick that chin in the air, you do your disciplining, and you bust a move out of there. Nothing says "like a boss" like calmly leading your screaming toddler out of the toy aisle where he's having a meltdown. You be the boss. There can only be one. And the minute they figure out this maxim is at all flexible, all havoc breaks loose. Do not test them. They can smell indecision at a country mile.*

14. *Fight the urge to rage against people who "promise to help" but don't. They will offer babysitting, meals, housecleaning, all in the name of goodwill and friendship. But when they don't come through (as people are wont to disappoint—and you're no exception), it is almost certainly because they are juggling their own load of kids and commitments. I am writing this while thinking of at least half a dozen promises I've neglected to keep. There are "babies" for whom I promised to*

deliver meals or presents who are now on their way to middle school. You yourself will let a lot of people down. Exhibit the grace you have so often been shown.

15. *An old Irish proverb says that a good laugh and a long sleep are the two best cures for anything. Watch your children carefully, because they will make you laugh every day. And it's impossible to survive motherhood without laughter. Your children will also make you cry. They will break your heart, mostly because their littleness is so captivating but so fleeting. They will also make you cry because all you want is that long Irish sleep, and for the next eighteen years you will never get it.*

16. *"Survival mode" is a code you and Matt will develop for the hard parts: when one of you is traveling, or someone is really sick, or the stretch of things running together is so hard you think you're never going to make it. In this mode, showers are optional, commitments are negligible, and vegetables are debatable. A daily outing sometimes works for nothing more than the simple fact no one can move when strapped in a car seat. It's all good, as long as everyone gets out on the other side alive.*

17. *During any given day, you'll be subjected to the endless feedback loop of: "Mom! Watch this!" "Mom! Look at me!" "Mom! Look what I can do!" What are they doing, you ask? Taking their first steps? Riding a bike for the first time? Splitting the atom? Sometimes, yes, it's a milestone moment. Other times, they just want you to see that they've figured out how to stand on one foot. But every time they call for you, it's a chance to show them that they're important. You validate them*

simply by watching them, by noticing them. Anyone can make children. Building children is daily work. Each time they ask you to watch them (even if you've seen their cannonball forty-two times), you prove they are important, that they have worth, and that what they're doing matters.

18. *On a Wednesday morning, in May 2013, you will be standing on a street corner in Washington, DC, with your husband. Four men in uniforms of light blue shirts and khaki pants will pass by, like some militarized suburbanites loosed from their white-collar jobs, headed to lunch. You will think to yourself that you remember these people, and the structure of a workday, and money. Yes, you certainly remember the money. Then your stomach will somersault with the remembered excitement of your children coming home from school and that you get to see them and douse them with embraces in just a few hours. You'll think then that these workers, or others like them in some workplace somewhere, will be waiting for you when the time is right. But then, on that street corner, all you'll be able to think about is getting home to see your kids.*

19. *When you're pulling a twelve-hour day prepping for a hearing, you're stuck at the office writing a proposal for a potential client, or you're facing a long line of irritated Christmas shoppers for whom you are the last stop before the holidays, remember this: motherhood is harder. You will not get a salary, a bonus, time off, or a promotion. You will be CEO, COO, accountant, HR manager, chef, concierge, and transportation coordinator. It is the ultimate long-term investment.*

So remember this, oh young one who is not forced to buy Pop Tarts on a bribe because Dad's not coming back for three more days: you will love it. You will live for it. Your children will get off the bus and come running to the car to see you like it is Christmas and you are Santa Claus. You will be their best friend, their first love, their confidante, and their biggest fan. When you are reunited with them after any absence, you will hug and kiss them as if there is no slaking your appetite for their embraces. It will be the only stage of your life out of which you will never grow or move on. This is a blessed reassurance, because you would never, ever want to.

Motherhood pays better than anything you'll ever do.

20. *Break's over.*

Hold up. . . . Do you smell something burning?

Notes

Chapter 1 Meet the Donners

1. Donald K. Grayson, "Donner Party Deaths: A Demographic Assessment," *Journal of Anthropological Research* 46 (Autumn 1990): 223–42.

2. Stephen McCurdy, "Epidemiology of Disaster: The Donner Party (1846–1847)," *Western Journal of Medicine* 160 (1994): 338–42.

3. John F. Helliwell, Richard Layard, and Jeffrey Sachs, eds., "World Happiness Report 2015," accessed May 12, 2015, www.worldhappiness.report.

4. Studs Terkel, *Working: People Talk about What They Do All Day and How They Feel about What They Do* (New York: The New Press, 1972), xiii.

Chapter 2 A Job Is a Job

1. Nora Ephron, *I Feel Bad about My Neck and Other Thoughts on Being a Woman* (New York: Vintage Books, 2006), 102.

2. Marc Bodnick, "Why Do So Many People Hate Their Jobs?" *Forbes*, March 27, 2013, http://www.forbes.com/sites/quora/2013/03/27/why-do-so-many-people-hate-their-jobs/.

3. Terkel, *Working*, xi.

4. "Ai Weiwei Zodiac Heads Sell for Record $4.3m in London," *Yahoo News*, February 15, 2015, http://news.yahoo.com/ai-weiwei-zodiac-heads-sell-record-4-3m-033416545.html;_ylt=A0LEVy4sA_pUj6UAzzJXNyoA;_ylu=X3oDMT EzbHRsbW41BGNvbG8DYmYxBHBvcwMxBHZ0aWQDVklQNTY4XzEEc 2VjA3Ny.

5. Glen Martin, "The Stay-at-Home Dilemma: Modern Dads Can Pay a Steep Price for Bonding with Baby," *California Magazine*, Winter 2014, http://alumni.berkeley.edu/california-magazine/winter-2014-gender-assumptions/stay-home-dilemma-modern-dads-can-pay-steep-price.

6. Ibid.

7. Jill Yavorsky, Claire Kamp Dush, and Sarah Schoppe-Sullivan, "The Origin of Gender Inequalities in Dual-Earner, College Educated Couples: The Division of Labor at the Transition to Parenthood," *Council on Contemporary Families*, May 7, 2015, https://contemporaryfamilies.org/origin-brief-report/.

8. "Profile America, Facts for Features," *US Census Bureau News*, March 9, 2012, http://www.census.gov/newsroom/releases/archives/facts_for_features_special _editions/cb12-ff08.html.

9. Alan Farnham, "Mother's Day: How Much Is Mom Worth?" *ABC News*, May 6, 2011, http://abcnews.go.com/Business/mothers-day-how-much-is-mom-worth /story?id=13545402.

10. "What Is a Mom's Work Worth?" Salary.com, accessed March 10, 2015, http://www.salary.com/mom-paycheck/.

Chapter 3 Look What I Can Do

1. Stephen King, *On Writing: A Memoir of the Craft* (New York: Pocket Books, 2002), 222.

Chapter 8 The Weirdos Next Door

1. Gwen Dewar, PhD, "Why Do You Want to Eat Your Baby?" Babycenter.com, September 25, 2013, http://blogs.babycenter.com/mom_stories/why-do-you-want -to-eat-your-baby/. See also Johan Lundstrom et al., "Maternal Status Regulates Cortical Responses to the Body Odor of Newborns," *Frontiers in Psychology*, September 5, 2013, http://journal.frontiersin.org/article/10.3389/fpsyg.2013.00597/full.

Chapter 9 Play Nice

1. Vanessa Grigoriadis, "'Primates of Park Avenue: A Memoir,' by Wednesday Martin: Sunday Book Review," *New York Times*, May 29, 2015, http://www .nytimes.com/2015/05/31/books/review/primates-of-park-avenue-a-memoir-by -wednesday-martin.html?_r=0.

2. Brigid Schulte, "Making Time for Kids? Study Says Quality Trumps Quantity," *Washington Post*, March 28, 2015, http://www.washingtonpost.com/local/making -time-for-kids-study-says-quality-trumps-quantity/2015/03/28/10813192-d378 -11e4-8fce-3941fc548f1c_story.html. See also Justin Wolfers, "Yes, Your Time As a Parent Does Make a Difference," *New York Times*, April 1, 2015, http:// www.nytimes.com/2015/04/02/upshot/yes-your-time-as-a-parent-does-make-a -difference.html.

3. Katharine Zaleski, "Female Company President: 'I'm Sorry to All the Mothers I Worked With,'" *Fortune*, March 3, 2015, http://fortune.com/2015/03/03 /female-company-president-im-sorry-to-all-the-mothers-i-used-to-work-with/.

Chapter 10 The Art of War

1. "Having Three Children Is Most Stressful for Mom, Survey Finds," *Huff Post Parents*, May 7, 2013, http://m.huffpost.com/us/entry/3229032.

2. See Gary Chapman, *The Five Love Languages* (Chicago: Northfield, 2015), http://www.5lovelanguages.com/faqs/love-languages/. The five love languages include physical touch, words of affirmation, quality time, acts of service, and gifts.

Chapter 12 I Feel Bad about My Brain

1. Lila Azam Zanganeh, "Umberto Eco, The Art of Fiction No. 197," *The Paris Review* 185 (Summer 2008), accessed August 1, 2015, http://www.theparisreview.org/interviews/5856/the-art-of-fiction-no-197-umberto-eco.

Chapter 13 Other People('s Children)

1. "Indian Toddler Dolly Sets National Archery Record," *The Times of India*, March 24, 2015, http://timesofindia.indiatimes.com/Sports/More-sports/Others/Indian-toddler-Dolly-sets-national-archery-record/articleshow/46677848.cms.

Chapter 14 The Continental Divide

1. Terkel, *Working*, 304.
2. Elisabeth Elliott, *Discipline: The Glad Surrender* (Grand Rapids: Revell, 2006), 126.

Chapter 15 The River of Stars

1. Michel de Montaigne, "Michel de Montaigne Quotes," *Goodreads*, accessed April 8, 2015, https://www.goodreads.com/author/quotes/17241.Michel_de_Montaigne.

Sarah Parshall Perry is a wife and mother of three children, which feels like a lot of kids even though it isn't. She has a BS in journalism from Liberty University and a JD from the University of Virginia School of Law. Sarah is the author of *Sand in My Sandwich: And Other Motherhood Messes I'm Learning to Love* (Revell, 2015), a contributing author to *The Horse of My Heart: Stories of the Horses We Love* (Revell, 2015), and coauthor of *When the Fairy Dust Settles: A Mother and Her Daughter Discuss What Really Matters* (FaithWords, 2004) with her mother, Janet Parshall. She is a contributor to multiple parenting blogs and the author of numerous magazine articles and award-winning short stories. Sarah has served in youth ministry for over ten years and works with the Family Research Council in Washington, DC. She lives in Baltimore, Maryland, where she is sometimes forced to hide in the closet to write.

VISIT

SarahPerryWrites.com

TO LEARN MORE

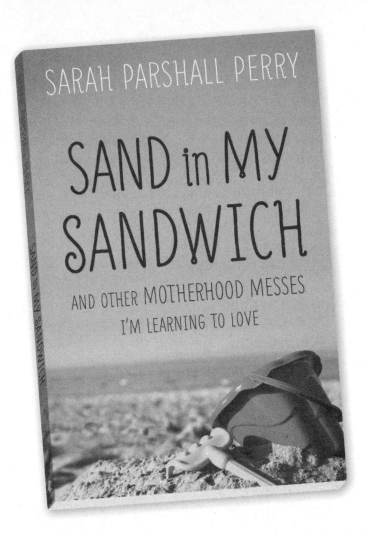

There is no perfect family, no life free of mess.
But in the midst of all of it, God is there,
reminding us, "My child, I got this."

YOU MAY ALSO ENJOY

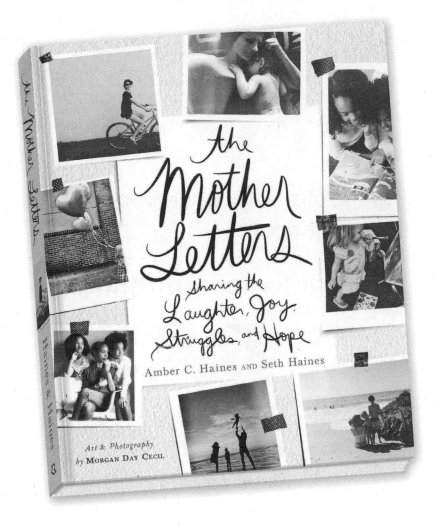

These wise, honest, and sometimes hilarious
letters are a beautiful collection of hope
and encouragement for moms everywhere.